THE DIVINE MILIEU

BY THE SAME AUTHOR

The Phenomenon of Man

PIERRE TEILHARD DE CHARDIN

THE DIVINE
MILIEU

AN ESSAY ON THE INTERIOR LIFE

HARPER & ROW, PUBLISHERS
NEW YORK AND EVANSTON

THE DIVINE MILIEU

English translation copyright © 1960 by Wm. Collins Sons &
Co., London, and Harper & Brothers, New York.

Printed in the United States of America

Originally published in French as Le Milieu Divin, copyright
1957 by Editions du Seuil, Paris.

This translation is published in Great Britain under the title
Le Milieu Divin.

E-M

Library of Congress catalog card number: 60-11787

"SIC DEUS DILEXIT MUNDUM" *

For those who love the world

CONTENTS

NOTE

Le Milieu Divin is volume four in Pierre Teilhard de Chardin's collected works as published in France, coming between *La Vision du Passé* and *L'Avenir de l'Homme*. In England and America it is volume two in the series, having been preceded by *The Phenomenon of Man* in 1959. If *The Phenomenon of Man* contained the kernel of Teilhard's scientific thought, *The Divine Milieu* is a key to the religious meditation that accompanied it.

All Teilhard's works involve grave problems for the translators, and the present version of *The Divine Milieu* is the result of much discussion and collaboration. Perhaps what most needs explanation is the retention of the word 'milieu' from the original French title. This has been done more by necessity than by choice. The word 'milieu' has no exact equivalent in English as it implies both centre and environment or setting: and even the normal use in England of the word 'milieu' has insular associations. One suggested title, 'In the Context of God,' did not meet with the approval of the French committee in charge of the publication of Teilhard's works and I myself did not feel that another, 'The Divine Environment,' was close enough to the original. As we could reach no agreed solution, we left the word 'milieu' in the title.

As a result of this, it was decided to retain the word 'milieu' throughout the text also. Readers are asked to understand this word in the precise French connotation in which it was used by the author.

BERNARD WALL

General Editor of the English edition
August, 1960   of the works of Teilhard de Chardin

PREFACE

If the form and content of the following pages are to be rightly understood, the reader must not misconceive the spirit in which they were written.

This book is not specifically addressed to Christians who are firmly established in their faith and have nothing more to learn about its beliefs. It is written for the waverers, both inside and outside; that is to say for those who, instead of giving themselves wholly to the Church, either hesitate on its threshold or turn away in the hope of surpassing it.

As a result of changes which, over the last century, have modified our experimental representations of the world and hence the moral value of many of its elements, the 'human religious ideal' inclines to stress certain tendencies and to express itself in terms which seem, at first sight, no longer to coincide with the 'Christian religious ideal.'

Thus it is that those whose education or instinct leads them to listen primarily to the voices of the earth, have a certain fear that they may be false to themselves or diminish themselves if they simply follow the Gospel path.

So the purpose of this Essay—on life or on inward vision—is to prove by a sort of tangible demonstration that this fear is unfounded, since the most traditional Christianity, expressed in Baptism, the Cross and the Eucharist, can be translated so as to embrace all that is best in the aspirations peculiar to our times.

My hope is that it may help to show that Christ, who is ever the same and ever new, has not ceased to be the 'first' within mankind.

An important observation

The following pages do not pretend to offer a complete treatise on ascetical theology—they only offer a simple *description* of a *psychological* evolution observed *over a specified interval.* A possible series of inward perspectives gradually revealed to the mind in the course of a humble yet 'illuminating' spiritual ascent—that is all we have tried to note down.

The reader need not, therefore, be surprised at the apparently small space allotted to moral evil and sin: the soul with which we are dealing is assumed to have already turned away from the path of error.

Nor should the fact arouse concern that the action of grace is not referred to or invoked more explicitly. The subject under consideration is actual, concrete 'supernaturalised' man—but seen in the realm of *conscious* psychology only. So there was no need to distinguish explicitly between natural and supernatural, between divine influence and human operation. But although the terms may be absent, the thing is everywhere taken for granted. Not only in the sense of a theoretically accepted entity, but also in the sense of a living reality, the notion of grace impregnates the whole atmosphere of my book.

And in fact *the divine milieu would lose all its grandeur and all its savour* for the 'mystic' if he did not feel—with his whole 'participated' being, with his whole soul gratuitously justified, with his whole will strengthened and encouraged—if he did not feel *so completely swept away* in the divine ocean that *no initial point of support* would be left him in the end, of his own, within himself, from which he could act.

INTRODUCTION

'In eo vivimus'

The enrichment and ferment of religious thought in our time has undoubtedly been caused by the revelation of the immensity and unity of the world all around us and within us. All around us the physical sciences are endlessly extending the abyss of time and space, and ceaselessly discerning new relationships between the elements of the universe. Within us a whole world of affinities and inter-related sympathies, as old as the human soul, is being awakened by the stimulus of these great discoveries, and what has hitherto been dreamed rather than experienced is at last taking shape and consistency. Scholarly and discriminated among serious thinkers, simple or didactic among the half-educated, these aspirations towards a vaster and more organic One, and the premonitions of unknown forces and their application in new fields, are the same, and are emerging simultaneously on all sides. It is almost a commonplace today to find men who, quite naturally and unaffectedly, live in the explicit consciousness of being an atom or a citizen of the universe.

This collective awakening, similar to that which, at some given moment, makes each individual realise the true dimensions of his own life, must inevitably have a profound religious reaction on the mass of mankind—either to cast down or to exalt.

To some, the world has disclosed itself as too vast: within such immensity, man is lost and no longer counts; and there is nothing left for him to do but shut his eyes and disappear. To others, the world is too beautiful; and it, and it alone, must be adored.

There are Christians, as there are men, who remain unaffected by these feelings of anxiety or fascination. The following pages are not for them. But there are others who are alarmed by the agitation or the attraction invincibly produced in them by this new rising star. Is the Christ of the Gospels, imagined and loved within the dimensions of a Mediterranean world, capable of still embracing and still forming the centre of our prodigiously expanded universe? Is the world not in the process of becoming more vast, more close, more dazzling than Jehovah? Will it not burst our religion asunder? Eclipse our God?

Without daring, perhaps, to admit to this anxiety yet, there are many (as I know from having come across them all over the world) who nevertheless feel it deep within them. It is for those that I am writing.

I shall not attempt to embark on metaphysics or apologetics. Instead, I shall turn back, with those who care to follow me, to the Agora. There, in each other's company, we shall listen to St. Paul telling the Areopagites of 'God, who made man that he might seek Him—God whom we try to apprehend in our tentative way—that self-same God is as out-stretched and tangible as the atmosphere in which we are bathed. He encompasses us on all sides, like the world itself. What prevents you, then, from enfolding Him in your arms? Only one thing: your inability *to see Him.*' [1]

[1] *Editor's Note.* At the end of his life the author reverted to *The Divine Milieu* in two autobiographical works where he expands what he means by *seeing Him:* 'Throughout my life, *through* my life, the world has little by little caught fire in my sight until, aflame all around me, it has become almost completely luminous from within . . . Such has been my experience in contact with the earth—the diaphany of the divine at the heart of the universe on fire . . . Christ; His heart; a fire: capable of penetrating everywhere and, gradually, spreading everywhere.'

This little book does no more than recapitulate the eternal lesson of the Church in the words of a man who, because he believes himself to feel deeply in tune with his own times, has sought to teach how to see God everywhere, to see Him in all that is most hidden, most solid and most ultimate in the world. These pages put forward no more than a practical attitude—or, more exactly perhaps, a way of teaching how to see. Let us begin by leaving argument aside for a moment. Place yourself here, where I am, and look from this privileged position —which is no hard-won height reserved for the elect, but the solid platform built by two thousand years of Christian experience—and you will see how easily the two stars, whose divergent attractions were disorganising your faith, are brought into conjunction. Without immixture, without confusion, the true God, the Christian God, will, under your gaze, invade the universe, our universe of today, the universe which so frightened you by its alarming size or its pagan beauty. He will penetrate it as a ray of light does a crystal; and, with the help of the great layers of creation, He will become for you universally tangible and active—very near and very distant at one and the same time.

If you are able to focus your soul's eyes so as to perceive this magnificence, you will soon forget, I assure you, your unfounded fears in face of the mounting significance of the earth. Your one thought will be to exclaim: *'Greater still, Lord, let your universe be greater still, so that I may hold You and be held by You by a ceaselessly widened and intensified contact!'*

The line we shall follow in our survey is quite simple. Since in the field of experience each man's existence can properly be divided into two parts—what he does and what he undergoes —we shall consider each of these parts in turn: the active and the passive. In each we shall find at the outset that, in accordance with His promise, God truly waits for us in things, unless indeed He comes to meet us. Next we shall marvel how the manifestation of His sublime presence in no way disturbs the harmony of our human attitude, but, on the contrary, brings it its true form and perfection. This done—that is, having shown that the two halves of our lives, and consequently the whole of our world, are full of God—it will remain for us to make an inventory of the wonderful properties of this milieu which is all around us (and which is nevertheless ulterior to everything), the only one in which, from now onwards, we are equipped to breathe freely.

PART ONE

THE DIVINISATION OF
OUR ACTIVITIES [1]

Of the two halves or components into which our lives may be divided, the most important, judging by appearances and by the price we set upon it, is the sphere of activity, endeavour and development. There can, of course, be no action without reaction. And, of course, there is nothing in us which in origin and at its deepest is not, as St. Augustine said, *'in nobis, sine nobis.'* When we act, as it seems, with the greatest spontaneity and vigour, we are to some extent led by the things we imagine we are controlling. Moreover, the very expansion of our energy (which reveals the core of our autonomous personality) is, ultimately, only our obedience to the will to be and to grow, of which we can master neither the variations of intensity nor the countless forms. We shall return, at the beginning of Part Two, to these essentially passive elements, some of which form part of the very marrow of our substance, while

---

[1] *Note.* It is of the utmost importance at this point to bear in mind what was said at the end of the Preface. We use the word 'activity' in the ordinary, current sense, without in any way denying—far from it— all that occurs between grace and the will in the infra-experimental spheres of the soul. To repeat: what is most divine in God is that, in an absolute sense, we are nothing apart from Him. The least admixture of what may be called Pelagianism would suffice to ruin immediately the beauties of the divine milieu in the eyes of the 'seer.'

others are diffused among the interplay of universal causes which we call our 'character,' our 'nature' or our 'good and bad luck.' For the moment let us consider our life in terms of the categories and definitions which are the most immediate and universal. Everyone can distinguish quite clearly between the moments in which he is acting and those in which he is acted upon. Let us look at ourselves in one of those phases of dominant activity and try to see how, with the help of our activity and by developing it to the full, the divine presses in upon us and seeks to enter our lives.

1. The Undoubted Existence of the Fact and the Difficulty of Explaining It. The Christian Problem of the Sanctification of Action

Nothing is more certain, dogmatically, than that human action can be sanctified. 'Whatever you do,' says St. Paul, 'do it in the name of Our Lord Jesus Christ.' And the dearest of Christian traditions has always been to interpret those words to mean: in intimate union with Our Lord Jesus Christ. St. Paul himself, after calling upon us to 'put on Christ,' goes on to forge the famous series of words *collaborare, compati, commori, con-resuscitare*, giving them the fullest possible meaning, a literal meaning even, and expressing the conviction that every human life must—in some sort—become a life in common with the life of Christ. The actions of life, of which we are speaking here, should not, as everyone knows, be understood solely in the sense of religious and devotional works (prayers, fasting, almsgiving). It is the whole of human life, down to its most 'natural' zones, which, the Church teaches, can be sanctified. 'Whether you eat or whether you drink,' St. Paul says. The whole history of the Church is there to attest it. Taken as a whole, then, from the most solemn declarations or examples of the Pontiffs and Doctors of the Church to the advice humbly given by the priest in confession, the general influence and practice of the Church has always been to dignify, ennoble and transfigure in God the duties inherent to one's station in life, the search for natural truth, and the development of human action.

The fact cannot be denied. But its legitimacy, that is its logical coherence with the whole basis of the Christian spirit, is not immediately apparent. How is it that the perspectives opened up by the Kingdom of God do not, by their very presence, shatter the equilibrium and economy of our activities? How can the man who believes in heaven and the Cross continue to believe seriously in the value of worldly occupations? How can the believer, in the name of everything that is most Christian in him, carry out his human duties to the fullest extent and as whole-heartedly and freely as if he were on the direct road to God? That is what is not altogether clear at first sight; and in fact disturbs more minds than one thinks.

The question might be put in this way:

According to the most sacred articles of his *Credo*, the Christian believes that life here below is continued in a life of which the joy, the suffering, the reality, are quite incommensurable with the present conditions in our universe. This contrast and disproportion are enough, by themselves, to rob us of our taste for the world and our interest in it; but to them must be added a positive doctrine of condemnation or contempt for a fallen and vitiated world. 'Perfection consists in detachment; the world about us is vanity and ashes.' The believer is constantly reading or hearing these austere words. How can he reconcile them with that other counsel, usually coming from the same master and in any case written in his heart by nature, that

he must be an example unto the Gentiles in devotion to duty,
in energy, and even in leadership in all the spheres opened
up by man's activity? There is no need for us to consider the
wayward or the lazy who cannot be bothered to acquire knowledge or organise a better life, from which they will benefit a
hundred-fold after their last breath, and only contribute to
the human task 'with the tips of their fingers' (to quote from
something once imprudently said). But there is a category of
mind (known to every spiritual director) for whom the difficulty takes the form and importance of a constant and paralysing perplexity. Such minds, set upon interior unity, become
the victims of a veritable spiritual dualism. On the one hand
a very sure instinct, mingled with their love of being and their
taste for life, draws them towards the joy of creation and knowledge. On the other hand a higher will to love God above all
else makes them afraid of the least division or deflection in
their allegiances. In the most spiritual layers of their being they
experience a tension between the opposing ebb and flow caused
by the attraction of the two rival stars we spoke of at the beginning: God and the world. Which of the two is to make itself
more nobly adored?

Depending on the greater or less vitality of the nature of
the individual, this conflict is in danger of finding its solution
in one of the three following ways: either the Christian will
repress his taste for the tangible and force himself to centre
his interest on purely religious objects only, trying to live in a
world made divine by the exclusion of the largest possible number of worldly objects; or else, harassed by that inward conflict which hampers him, he will dismiss the evangelical
counsels and decide to lead what seems to him a complete
and human life; or else, again, and this is the most usual case,
he will give up any attempt to understand; he will never belong
wholly to God, nor ever wholly to things; imperfect in his own

eyes, and insincere in the eyes of men, he will become resigned
to leading a double life. I am speaking, it should not be forgotten, from experience.

For various reasons, all three of these solutions are dangerous.
Whether we become distorted, disgusted or divided, the result
is equally bad, and certainly contrary to that which Christianity
should rightly produce in us. There is, without possible doubt,
a fourth way out of the problem: it consists in seeing how,
without making the smallest concession to 'nature' but with
a desire for greater perfection, we can reconcile, and provide
mutual nourishment for, the love of God and a healthy love of
the world, a striving towards detachment and a striving towards
development.

Let us look at the two solutions that can be brought to the
Christian problem of 'the divinisation of human activity,' the
first partial, the second complete.

2. An Incomplete Solution: Human Action Has No Value Other Than the Intention Which Directs It

Reduced somewhat crudely and schematically to essentials, the
immediate answer given by spiritual directors to those who ask
them how a Christian who is determined to despise the world
and jealously reserve his heart for God, can love what he is
doing (his work)—in conformity with the Church's teaching
that the faithful should take *not a lesser* but a *fuller* part than
the pagan—may be put thus:

'You are anxious, my friend, to restore the value of your
human endeavour which seems to you to be depreciated by the
Christian vision and Christian asceticism. Very well then, pour

over it the marvellous substance of good will. Purify your intention, and the least of your actions will be filled with God.
No doubt the material side of your actions has no ultimate
value. Whether men discover one truth or one fact more or
less, whether or not they make beautiful music or beautiful
pictures, whether their organisation of the world is more or
less successful—all that has no direct importance for heaven.
None of these discoveries or creations will become one of the
stones from which is built the New Jerusalem. But what will
count, up there, what will always endure, is this: that you have
acted in all things *conformably* to the will of God.

'God obviously has no need of the products of your busy
activity, since He could give Himself everything without you.
The only thing that interests Him, the one thing He desires
intensely, is the faithful use of your freedom, and the prefer-
ence you accord Him over the things around you.

'Try to grasp this: the things which are given to you on earth
are given you purely as an exercise, a 'blank sheet' on which
you make your own mind and heart. You are on a testing-
ground where God can judge whether you are capable of being
translated to heaven and into His presence. You are on trial.
So that it matters very little what becomes of the fruits of the
earth, or what they are worth. The whole question is whether
you have used them in order to learn how to obey and how
to love.

'You should not, therefore, cling to the coarse outer-covering
of human activities: these are but inflammable straw or brittle
clay. But try to realise that into each of these humble vessels
you can pour, like a sap or a precious liquid, the spirit of obedience and of union with God. If worldly aims have no value in
themselves, you can love them for the opportunity they give
you of proving your constancy to God.'

We are not suggesting that the foregoing words are ever

actually used; but we believe they convey a shade of meaning which is often present in spiritual advice, and we are sure that they give a rough idea of what a good number of the 'directed' have understood and retained of the exhortations given them.

On this assumption let us examine the attitude which they recommend.

In the first place this attitude contains an enormous part of truth. It rightly exalts the initial and basic role of intention which is really (as we shall have occasion to repeat) the golden key by which the inward world is opened to the divine Presence. It expresses vigorously the substantial value of the divine will which, by virtue of this attitude, becomes for the Christian (as it was for his divine Model) the life-giving marrow of all earthly nourishment. It reveals a sort of unique milieu, unchanging beneath the diversity and plurality of human works, in which we can settle without ever having to leave it.

These various features are a primary and essential approximation to the solution we are looking for; and we shall certainly retain them in their entirety in the more satisfactory plan of the interior life which will soon be suggested. But they seem to us to lack the fulfilment which our spiritual peace and joy so imperiously demand. The divinisation of our endeavour by the value of the intention put into it infuses a precious soul into all our actions; but *it does not confer the hope of resurrection upon their bodies.* Yet that hope is what we need if our joy is to be complete. It is certainly a very great thing to be able to think that, if we love God, something of our inner activity, of our *operatio*, will never be lost. But will not the work itself of our minds, of our hearts and of our hands—that is to say, our achievements, our products, our *opus*—will not this, too, in some sense be 'eternalised' and saved?

Indeed, Lord, it will be—by virtue of a need which You

Yourself have implanted at the very centre of my will! I desire and need that it should be.

I desire it because I love irresistibly all that your continuous help enables me to bring each day to reality. A thought, a material improvement, a harmony, a particular expression of love, the enchanting complexity of a smile or a look, all the new beauties that appear for the first time, in me or around me, on the human face of the earth—I cherish them like children and cannot believe that they will die entirely in the flesh. If I believed that these things were to wither away for ever, should I have given them life? The more I examine myself, the more I discover this psychological truth: that no one lifts his little finger to do the smallest task unless moved, however obscurely, by the conviction that he is contributing infinitesimally (at least indirectly) to the construction of some absolute—that is to say, to Your work, my God. This may well sound strange or exaggerated to those who act without thoroughly analysing themselves. And yet it is a fundamental law of their action. It requires no less than the attraction of what is called the Absolute, no less than You Yourself, to set in motion the frail liberty with which You have endowed us. And that being so, everything which diminishes my explicit faith in the heavenly value of the results of my endeavour, lowers irremediably my power to act.

Show all Your faithful, Lord, in what a full and true sense 'their work follows them' into Your Kingdom—opera sequuntur illos. Otherwise they will become like those idle labourers who are not spurred by their task. Or, if human instinct triumphs over their hesitations or the sophisms of a religion upon which not sufficient light has been thrown, they will remain fundamentally divided and frustrated; and it will be said that the sons of heaven cannot compete on the human level, in conviction and hence on equal terms, with the children of the world.

3. The Final Solution: All Endeavour Cooperates to Complete the World 'In Christo Jesu'

The general economy of the salvation (which is to say the divinisation) of our works can be expressed briefly in the following syllogism.

At the heart of our universe, each soul exists for God, in
Our Lord.

But all reality, even material reality, around each one of us,
exists for our souls.

Hence, all sensible reality, around each one of us, exists,
through our souls, for God in Our Lord.

Let us examine each term of the syllogism in turn and sepa-
rately. Its terms and the link between them are easy to grasp.
But we must beware: it is one thing to have understood its
words, and another to have penetrated the astonishing world
whose inexhaustible riches are revealed by its calm precision.

A. At the heart of our universe, each soul exists for God, in Our Lord

The major of the syllogism does no more than express the
fundamental Catholic dogma, which all other dogmas merely
explain or define. It therefore requires no proof here; but it
does need to be strictly understood by the intelligence. Each
soul exists for God in Our Lord. We should not be content to
give this destination of our being in Christ a meaning too
slavishly imitative of the legal relationship which in our world
links an object to its owner. Its nature is altogether more physical and deeper. Because the consummation of the world (the
Pleroma, as St. Paul says) is a communion of persons (the

Communion of Saints), our minds no doubt require that we
should express the relationship with the help of analogies drawn
from society. Moreover, in order to avoid the perverse pantheism and materialism which lie in wait for our thought whenever
it applies to its mystical concepts the powerful but dangerous
resources of analogies drawn from organic life, the majority of
theologians (more cautious on this point than St. Paul) do
not favour too literal an interpretation of the links which bind
the limbs to the Head in the Mystical Body. But there is no
reason why caution should become timidity. If we want a full
and vivid understanding of the teachings of the Church (which
alone makes them beautiful and acceptable) on the value of
human life and the promises or threats of the future life—then,
without rejecting anything of the forces of freedom and of
consciousness which form the physical reality proper to the human soul, we must perceive the existence of links between us
and the Incarnate Word no less precise than those which control, in the world, the affinities of the elements in the building
up of 'natural' wholes.

There is no point, here, in seeking a new name by which to
designate the supreme nature of that dependence, where all
that is most flexible in human combinations and all that is
most intransigent in organic structures, merge harmoniously in
a paroxysm. We will continue to call it by the name that has
always been used: *mystical* union. Far from implying some idea
of attenuation, we use the term to mean the strengthening and
purification of the reality and urgency contained in the most
powerful interconnections revealed to us in every order of the
physical and human world. On that path we can advance without fear of over-stepping the truth; for everyone in the Church
of God is agreed upon the fact itself, if not upon its systematic
statement: by virtue of the powerful Incarnation of the Word,
our soul is wholly dedicated to Christ and centred upon Him.

B. 'In our universe,' we went on to say, 'in which each soul goes to God, in Our Lord, all that is sensible, in its turn, exists for the soul'

In the form in which we have given it, the minor of our syllogism is tinged with a certain finalism which may shock those with a positivist cast of mind. Nevertheless it does no more than express an incontrovertible natural fact—which is that our spiritual being is continually nourished by the countless energies of the tangible world. Here, again, proof is unnecessary. But it is essential to see—to see things as they are and to see them really and intensely. We live at the centre of the network of cosmic influences as we live at the heart of the human crowd or among the myriads of stars, without, alas, being aware of their immensity. If we wish to live our humanity and our Christianity to the full, we must overcome that lack of sensibility which tends to conceal things from us in proportion as they are too close to us or too vast. It is worth while performing the salutary exercise which consists in starting from the most personalised zones of our consciousness and following the prolongations of our being throughout the world. We shall be astonished at the extent and the intimacy of our relationship with the universe.

Where are the roots of our being? In the first place they plunge back and down into the unfathomable past. How great is the mystery of the first cells which were one day animated by the breath of our souls! How impossible to decipher the synthesis of successive influences in which we are for ever incorporated! In each one of us, through matter, the whole history of the world is in part reflected. And however autonomous our soul, it is heir to an existence worked upon from all sides—before it came into being—by the totality of the energies of

the earth: it meets and rejoins life at a determined level. Then,
hardly has it entered actively into the universe at that particular
point than it feels, in its turn, besieged and penetrated by the
flow of cosmic influences which have to be ordered and assimilated. Let us look around us: the waves come from all
sides and from the farthest horizon. Through every cleft the
sensible world inundates us with its riches—food for the body,
nourishment for the eyes, harmony of sounds and fulness of
the heart, unknown phenomena and new truths, all these treasures, all these urges, all these calls, coming from the four quar-
ters of the world, pass through our consciousness at every
moment. What is their role within us? What will their effect be,
even if we receive them passively or indistinctly, like bad work-
men? They will merge into the most intimate life of our soul,
and either develop it or poison it. We only have to look at
ourselves for one moment to realise this, and feel either delight
or anxiety. If even the most humble and most material of our
nourishment is capable of deeply influencing our most spiritual
faculties, what can be said of the infinitely more penetrating
energies conveyed to us by the music of tones, of notes, of
words, of ideas? We have not, in us, a body to be nourished
independently of our soul. Everything that the body has ad-
mitted and has begun to transform must be sublimated by the
soul in its turn. The soul does this, no doubt, in its own way
and with its own dignity. But it cannot escape from this universal contact nor from that unremitting labour. And that is
how the characteristic power of understanding and loving,
which will form its immaterial individuality, is gradually per-
fected in it for its own good and at its own risk. We hardly
know in what proportions and under what guise our natural
faculties will pass over into the final act of the divine vision.
But it can hardly be doubted that, with God's help, it is here
below that we give ourselves the eyes and the heart which a

final transfiguration will transmute into organs of a capacity
for adoration and beatification special to each one of us.

The masters of the spiritual life continue to repeat that God
wants only souls. To give those words their true value, we must
not forget that the human soul, however independently created
our philosophy imagines it to be, is inseparable, in its birth
and in its growth, from the universe into which it is born. In
each soul, God loves and partly saves the whole world which
that soul sums up in an incommunicable and particular way.
Now this summing-up, this synthesis is not given to us ready-
made and complete with the first awakening of consciousness.
It is we who, through our own activity, must industriously as-
semble the widely scattered elements. The labour of seaweed
as it concentrates in its tissues the substances dispersed, in infinitesimal quantities, throughout the vast layers of the ocean;
the industry of bees as they make honey from the juices scattered in so many flowers—these are but pale images of the
continuous process of elaboration which all the forces of the
universe undergo in us in order to become spirit.

Thus every man, in the course of his life, must not only show
himself obedient and docile. By his fidelity he must *construct*—
starting from the most natural zone of his own self—a work,
an *opus*, into which something enters from all the elements
of the earth. *He makes his own soul* throughout all his earthly
days; and at the same time he collaborates in another work,
in another *opus*, which infinitely transcends, while at the same
time it narrowly determines, the perspectives of his individual
achievement: the completion of the world. For in presenting
the Christian doctrine of salvation, it must not be forgotten
that the world, taken as a whole, that is to say in so far as it
constitutes a hierarchy of souls—which appear only successively,
develop only collectively and will be completed only in union—
the world, too, undergoes a sort of vast 'ontogenesis' in which

the development of each soul, assisted by sensible realities, is
but a diminished harmonic. Beneath our individual strivings towards spiritualisation, the world slowly accumulates, starting
with the whole of matter, that which will make of it the Heavenly Jerusalem or the New Earth.

*C. We can now bring together the major and minor
of our syllogism so as to grasp the link between them
and the conclusion*

If it is true, as we know from the Creed, that souls pass so
intimately into Christ and God, and if it is true, as we know
from the most general conclusions of psycho-analysis, that the
sensible passes vitally into the most spiritual zones of our souls
—then we must also recognise that in the whole process which
from first to last activates and directs the elements of the universe, *everything forms a single whole.* And we begin to see
more distinctly the great sun of Christ the King, of Christ
amictus mundo, of the universal Christ, rising over our interior
world. Little by little, stage by stage, everything is finally linked
to the supreme Centre *in quo omnia constant.* The emanations
coming from this Centre operate not only within the higher
zones of the world, where human activities take place in a
distinctively supernatural and meritorious form. In order to save
and constitute these sublime energies, the power of the Incarnate Word penetrates matter itself; it descends into the
deepest depths of the inferior forces. And the Incarnation will
be complete only when the part of chosen substance contained
in every object—spiritualised first of all in our souls and a second
time with our souls in Jesus—has rejoined the final Centre of
its completion. *Quid est quod ascendit, nisi quod prius descendit, ut repleret omnia.*

It is through the collaboration which He stimulates in us

that Christ, starting from *all* created things, is consummated and attains His plenitude. St. Paul himself tells us so. We may, perhaps, imagine that the Creation was finished long ago. But that would be quite wrong. It continues still more magnificently, and in the highest zones of the world. *Omnis creatura adhuc ingemiscit et parturit.* And we serve to complete it, even by the humblest work of our hands. That is, ultimately, the meaning and value of our acts. Owing to the inter-relation between matter, soul and Christ, we lead part of the being which He desires back to God *in whatever we do.* With each one of our *works,* we labour—atomically, but no less really—to build the Pleroma; that is to say, we bring to Christ a little fulfilment.

4. Communion through Action

Each one of our works, by its more or less remote or direct repercussion upon the spiritual world, contributes to perfect Christ in His mystical totality. That is the fullest possible answer to the question: How can we, following the call of St. Paul, see God in all the active half of our lives? In fact, through the unceasing operation of the Incarnation, the divine so thoroughly permeates all our creaturely energies that, in order to encounter and embrace it, we could not find a more appropriate milieu than that of our action.

To begin with, in action I cleave to the creative power of God; I co-incide with it; I become not only its instrument but its living prolongation. And since there is nothing more personal in a being than its will, I merge myself, in a sense, through my heart, with the very heart of God. This contact is continuous because I am always acting; and at the same time, since I can never find a limit to the perfection of my fidelity

or the fervour of my intention, it enables me to assimilate myself still more narrowly, and indefinitely, to God.

The soul does not pause to enjoy this communion, nor does
it lose sight of the material end of its action; it is wedded to
a *creative* effort. The will to succeed, a certain passionate delight in the work to be done, form an integral part of our
creaturely fidelity. It follows that the very sincerity with which
we desire and pursue success for God reveals itself as a new
factor—also without limits—in our more perfect conjunction
with the All-powerful who animates us. Originally associated
with God in the simple common exercise of wills, we now unite
ourselves to Him in a common love of the end for which we
are working; and the crowning marvel is that, with the possession of this end, we have the utter joy of discovering His presence once again.

All this follows directly from what was said a moment back
on the relationship between natural and supernatural actions
in the world. Any increase that I can confer upon myself or
upon things is translated into some increase in my power to
love and some progress in Christ's blessed hold upon the universe. Our work appears to us in the main as a way of earning
our daily bread. But its essential virtue is of a higher order:
through it we complete in ourselves the subject of the divine
union; and through it again we augment in some sense, in relation to ourselves, the divine end of that union, Our Lord Jesus
Christ. Hence whatever our human function may be, whether
artist or working-man or scholar, we can, if we are Christians,
speed towards the object of our work as though towards an
outlet open on the supreme fulfilment of our beings. Indeed,
without exaggeration or excess in thought or expression—but
simply by confronting the most fundamental truths of our faith
and of experience—we are led to the following observation: God
is inexhaustibly attainable in the *totality* of our action. And

this prodigy of divinisation is only comparable to the gentleness with which the metamorphosis is accomplished, without disturbing in any way (*non minuit, sed sacravit* . . .) the perfection and unity of human endeavour.

5. The Christian Perfection of Human Endeavour

There was reason to fear, as we have said, that the introduction of Christian perspectives might seriously upset the economy of human action; that the seeking after, and expectation of, the Kingdom of Heaven might deflect human activity from its natural tasks, or at least entirely eclipse any interest in them. Now we see why this cannot and must not be so. The conjunction of God and the world has just taken place under our eyes in the domain of action. No, God does not deflect our gaze prematurely from the work He Himself has given us, since He presents Himself to us as attainable through that very work. Nor does He blot out, in His intense light, the detail of our earthly aims, since the intimacy of our union with Him is in fact a function of the exact fulfilment of the least of our tasks. We ought to accustom ourselves to this basic truth till we are steeped in it, until it becomes as familiar to us as the perception of relief or the reading of words. God, in all that is most living and incarnate in Him, is not withdrawn from us beyond the tangible sphere; He is waiting for us at every moment in our action, in our work of the moment. He is in some sort at the tip of my pen, my spade, my brush, my needle—of my heart and of my thought. By pressing the stroke, the line, or the stitch, on which I am engaged, to its ultimate natural finish, I shall arrive at the ultimate aim towards which my innermost will tends. Like those formidable physical forces which man contrives to discipline so as to make them perform operations of prodigious delicacy, so the tremendous power of the divine attraction is focused on our frail desires and microscopic intents without breaking their point. It sur-animates; hence it neither disturbs anything nor stifles anything. It sur-animates; hence it introduces a higher principle of unity into our spiritual life, the specific effect of which is—depending upon the point of view one adopts—either to sanctify human endeavour or to humanise the Christian life.

A. *The sanctification of human endeavour*

I do not think I am exaggerating when I say that nine out of ten practicing Christians feel that man's work is always at the level of a 'spiritual encumbrance.' In spite of the practice of right intentions, and the day offered every morning to God, the general run of the faithful dimly feel that time spent at the office or the studio, in the fields or in the factory, is time diverted from prayer and adoration. It is impossible not to work —that is taken for granted. But it is impossible, too, to aim at the deep religious life reserved for those who have the leisure to pray or preach all day long. A few moments of the day can be salvaged for God, yes, but the best hours are absorbed, or at any rate cheapened, by material cares. Under the sway of this feeling, large numbers of Catholics lead a double or crippled life in practice: they have to step out of their human dress so as to have faith in themselves as Christians—and inferior Christians at that.

What has been said above of the divine extensions and divine requirements of the mystical or universal Christ should be enough to demonstrate both the invalidity of these impressions and the legitimacy of the thesis (so dear to Christianity) of

sanctification through the duties of our station in life. There
are, of course, certain noble and cherished moments of the day
—those when we pray or receive the sacraments. But for these
moments of more efficient or more explicit contact, the tide
of the divine omnipresence, and our perception of it, would
weaken until all that was best in our human endeavour, without
being entirely lost to the world, would be for us emptied of
God. But once we have jealously safeguarded our relation to
God encountered, if I may dare use the expression, 'in a pure
state' (that is to say in a state of Being distinct from all the
elements of this world), there is no need to fear that the most
banal, absorbing or attractive of occupations should force us
to depart from Him. To repeat: by virtue of the Creation and,
still more, of the Incarnation, *nothing* here below *is profane*
for those who know how to see. On the contrary, everything is
sacred to those capable of distinguishing that portion of chosen
being which is subject to the attraction of Christ in the process
of consummation. Try, with God's help, to perceive the connection—even physical and natural—which binds your labour
with the building of the Kingdom of Heaven; try to realise that
heaven itself smiles upon you and, through your works, draws
you to itself; then, as you leave church for the noisy streets,
you will remain with only one feeling, that of continuing to
immerse yourself in God. If your work is dull or exhausting,
take refuge in the inexhaustible and becalming interest of progressing in the divine life. If your work enthrals you, then allow
the spiritual impulse which matter communicates to you to
enter into your taste for God whom you know better and desire
more under the veil of His works. Never, at any time, 'whether
eating or drinking,' consent to do anything without first of all
realising its significance and constructive value *in Christo Jesu,*
and pursuing it with all your might. This is not simply a commonplace precept for salvation: it is the very path to sanctity

for each man according to his state and calling. For what is sanctity in a creature if not to cleave to God with the maximum of his strength? and what does that maximum cleaving to God mean if not the fulfilment—in the world organised around Christ—of the exact function, be it lowly or eminent, to which that creature is destined both by nature and by supernature?

Within the Church we observe all sorts of groups whose members are vowed to the perfect practice or this or that particular virtue: mercy, detachment, the splendour of the liturgy, the missions, contemplation. Why should there not be men vowed to the task of exemplifying, by their lives, the general sanctification of human endeavour?—men whose common religious ideal would be to give a full and conscious explanation of the divine possibilities or demands which any worldly occupation implies—men, in a word, who would devote themselves, in the fields of thought, art, industry, commerce and politics, etc., to carrying out, in the sublime spirit these demand, the basic tasks which form the very bonework of human society? Around us the 'natural' progress which nourishes the sanctity of each new age is all too often left to the children of the world, that is to say to agnostics or the irreligious. Unconsciously or involuntarily, no doubt, these collaborate in the Kingdom of God and in the fulfilment of the elect: their efforts, transcending or correcting their incomplete or bad intentions, are gathered in by Him 'whose energy subjects all things to itself.' But that is no more than a second best, a temporary phase in the organisation of human activity. Right from the hands that knead the dough, to those that consecrate it, the great and universal Host should be prepared and handled in a spirit of *adoration*.

May the time come when men, having been awakened to a sense of the close bond linking all the movements of this world in the unique work of the Incarnation, shall be unable to give themselves to a single one of their tasks without illuminating it with the clear vision that their work—however elementary it may be—is received and made use of by a Centre of the universe.

When that comes to pass, there will be little to separate life in the cloister from the life of the world. And only then will the action of the children of heaven (at the same time as the action of the children of the world) have attained the intended plenitude of its humanity.

B. *The humanisation of Christian endeavour*

The great objection brought against Christianity in our time, and the real source of the distrust which insulates entire blocks of humanity from the influence of the Church, has nothing to do with historical or theological difficulties. It is the suspicion that our religion makes its adherents *inhuman*.

'Christianity,' so some of the best of the Gentiles are inclined to think, 'is bad or inferior because it does not lead its followers beyond humanity, but away from it or to one side of it. It isolates them instead of merging them with the mass. Instead of harnessing them to the common task, it causes them to lose interest in it. Hence far from exalting them, it diminishes and distorts them. Moreover don't they admit as much themselves? And if one of their religious, or one of their priests, should happen to devote his life to what is called profane research, he is very careful, as a rule, to recall that he only lends himself to these secondary pursuits for the sake of conforming to a fashion or an illusion, to prove that Christians are not the most stupid of men. When a Catholic works with us, we invariably get the impression that he is doing so in an insincere way, condescendingly. He appears to be interested, but in fact, be-

cause of his religion, he does not believe in the human effort.
His heart is not really with us. Christianity creates deserters
and false friends: that is what we cannot forgive.'

We have placed this objection, which would be mortal if it
were true, in the mouth of an unbeliever. But has it no echo,
here and there, within the most faithful souls? What Christian
who has become aware of a sheet of glass insulating him
from his non-believing colleagues, has not asked himself uneasily
whether he was not on a false tack or had not actually lost
touch with the main current of mankind?

Without denying that some Christians, by their words more
than their deeds, do give grounds for the reproach of being,
if not the 'enemies,' at least the 'laggards' of the human race,
we can safely assert, after what we said above concerning the
supernatural value of our work on earth, that their attitude is
due to an incomplete understanding and not at all to some
greater perfection of religion.

How could we be deserters, or sceptical about the future of
the tangible world? How could we be repelled by human labour?
How little you know us! You suspect us of not sharing your
concern and your hopes and your exaltation at the penetration
of mysteries and the conquest of the forces of nature. 'Emotions
of this kind,' you say, 'can only be shared by men struggling
side by side for existence; whereas you Christians profess to be
saved already.' As though for us as for you, indeed far more
than for you, it were not a matter of life and death that the
earth should flourish to the uttermost of its natural powers. As
far as you are concerned (and it is here that you are not yet
human enough, you do not *go to the limits* of your humanity)
it is simply a matter of the success or failure of a reality which
remains vague and precarious even when conceived in the form
of some super-humanity. For us it is a question in a true sense

of achieving the victory of no less than a God. One thing is
infinitely disappointing, I grant you: far too many Christians
are insufficiently conscious of the 'divine' responsibilities of
their lives, and live like other men, giving only half of themselves, never experiencing the spur or the intoxication of further-
ing the Kingdom of God in every domain of mankind. But do
not blame anything but our weakness: our faith imposes on us
the right and the duty to throw ourselves into the things of
the earth. As much as you, and even better than you (because,
of the two of us, I alone am in a position to prolong the perspectives of my endeavour to infinity, in conformity with the
requirements of my present intention) I want to dedicate myself body and soul to the sacred duty of research. We must test
every barrier, try every path, plumb every abyss. *Nihil intentatum* . . . God wills it, who willed that He should have need
of it. You are men, you say? *Plus et ego.*

Plus et ego. There can be no doubt of it. At a time when the
consciousness of its own powers and possibilities is legitimately
awakening in a mankind now ready to become adult, one of
the first apologetic duties of the Christian is to show, by the
logic of his religious views and still more by the logic of his
action, that the Incarnate God did not come to diminish the
magnificent responsibility and splendid ambition that is ours:
of becoming our own self. Once again, *non minuit, sed sacravit.*
No, Christianity is not, as it is sometimes presented and sometimes practised, an additional burden of observances and obli-
gations to weigh down and increase the already heavy load, or
to multiply the already paralysing ties of social life. It is, in
fact, a soul of immense power which bestows significance and
beauty and a new lightness on what we are already doing. It is
true that it sets us on the road towards unsuspected heights.
But the slope which leads to these heights is linked so closely

with the one we were already climbing naturally, that there is
nothing so distinctively human in the Christian (and this is
what remains to be considered) as his detachment.

6. Detachment through Action

There hardly seems room for any dispute between Christians
about what we have so far said about the *intrinsic* divinisation
of human endeavour, since we have confined ourselves, in establishing it, to taking, in their proper strict sense, certain universally recognised theoretical and practical truths and confronting them with each other.

Nevertheless, some readers, though without finding any specific flaw in our argument, may feel vaguely upset or uneasy
in the face of a Christian ideal which lays such stress on the
preoccupations of human development and the pursuit of
earthly improvements. They should bear in mind that we are
still only half way along the road which leads to the mountain
of the Transfiguration. Up to this point we have been dealing
only with the active part of our lives. In a moment or two, when
we come to the chapter on passivities and diminishment, the
arms of the Cross will begin to dominate the scene more widely.
Let us consider it for a moment. In the very optimistic and
very broadening attitude which has been roughly sketched above,
a true and deep renunciation lies concealed. Anyone who de-
votes himself to human duty, according to the Christian formula, though outwardly he may seem to be immersed in the
concerns of the earth, is in fact, down to the depths of his being,
a man of great detachment.

Of its very nature, work is a multiple factor in detachment,
provided a man gives himself to it faithfully and without re-

bellion. In the first place it implies effort and a victory over inertia. And then, however interesting and intellectual it may be (and the more intellectual it is, the truer this becomes) work is always accompanied by the painful pangs of birth. Man can escape the terrible boredom of monotonous and commonplace duty only by facing the inner tension and the anxieties of 'creation.' To create, or organise material energy, or truth, or beauty, brings with it an inner torment which prevents those who face its hazards from sinking into the quiet and closed-in life wherein grows the vice of egoism and attachment. An honest workman not only surrenders his tranquillity and peace once and for all, but must learn to abandon over and over again the form which his labour or art or thought first took, and go in search of new forms. To pause, so as to enjoy or possess results, would be a betrayal of action. Over and over again he must transcend himself, tear himself away from himself, leaving behind him his most cherished beginnings. And on that road, which is not so different from the royal road of the Cross as might appear at first sight, detachment does not consist only in continually replacing one object with another of the same order—as miles, on a flat road, replace miles. By virtue of a marvellous mounting force contained in things (and which will be analysed in greater detail when we consider the 'spiritual power of matter'), each reality attained and left behind gives us access to the discovery and pursuit of an ideal of higher spiritual content. Those who spread their sails in the right way to the winds of the earth will always find themselves borne by a current towards the highest seas. The more nobly a man wills and acts, the more avid he becomes for great and sublime aims to pursue. He will no longer be content with family, country and the remunerative aspect of his work. He will want wider organisations to create, new paths to blaze, causes to uphold, truths to discover, an ideal to nourish and defend. So, gradually the worker no longer belongs to himself. Little by little the great breath of the universe has insinuated itself into him through the fissure of his humble but faithful action, has broadened him, raised him up, borne him on.

It is in the Christian, provided he knows how to make the most of the resources of his faith, that these effects will reach their climax and their crown. As we have seen: from the point of view of the reality, accuracy and splendour of the ultimate end towards which we must aim in the least of our acts, we, disciples of Christ, are the most favoured of men. The Christian knows that his function is to divinise the world in Jesus Christ. In him, therefore, the natural process which drives human action from ideal to ideal and towards objects ever more consistent and universal, reaches—thanks to the support of revelation—its fullest expansion. And in him, consequently, detachment through action should produce its maximum effectiveness.

And this is perfectly true. The Christian as we have described him in these pages, is at once the most attached and the most detached of men. Convinced in a way in which the 'worldly' cannot be of the unfathomable importance and value concealed beneath the humblest worldly successes, the Christian is at the same time as convinced as the hermit of the worthlessness of any success which is envisaged only as a personal advantage (or even a general one) without reference to God. It is God and God alone whom he pursues through the reality of created things. For him, interest lies truly *in* things, but in absolute dependence upon God's presence in them. The light of heaven becomes tangible and attainable to him through the crystal of beings. But he wants only this light, and if the light is extinguished, whether because the object is displaced, surpassed, or displaces itself, then even the most precious substance is only ashes in his sight. So that in himself and in his most personal development, it is not himself that he is seeking, but that which is greater than he, to which he knows that he is destined. In his own view he himself no longer counts, no longer exists; he has forgotten and lost himself in the very endeavour which is making him perfect. It is no longer the atom which lives, but the universe within it.

Not only has he encountered God in the entire field of his tangible activities, but in the course of this first phase of his spiritual development, the divine milieu which has been uncovered absorbs his powers in the very proportion in which these laboriously rise above their individuality.

PART TWO

THE DIVINISATION OF
OUR PASSIVITIES

While man by the very development of his powers is led to discover ever vaster and higher aims for his action, he also tends to be dominated by the object of his conquests and, like Jacob wrestling with the Angel, he ends by adoring what he was struggling against. The magnitude which he has unveiled and unleashed brings him into subjection. And then, because of his nature as element, he is brought to recognise that, in the final act that is to unite him to the All, the two terms of the union are utterly disproportionate. He, the lesser, has to receive rather than to give. He finds himself in the grip of what he thought he could grasp.

The Christian, who is by right the first and most human of men, is more subject than others to this psychological reversal whereby, in the case of all intelligent creatures, joy in action imperceptibly melts into desire for submission, and the exaltation of becoming one's own self into the zeal to die in another. Having been perhaps primarily alive to the attractions of union with God through action, he begins to conceive and then to desire a complementary aspect, an ulterior phase, in his communion: one in which he would not develop himself so much as lose himself in God.

He does not have to look far to discover possibilities and

opportunities for fulfilment in this gift of self. They are offered him at every moment—indeed they besiege him on all sides in the length and depth of the countless servitudes which make us servants far more than masters of the universe.

The moment has come to examine the number, the nature, and the possible divinisation of our passivities.

1. The Extent, Depth and Diverse Forms of Human Passivities

The passivities of our lives, as we said at the beginning of this study, form half of human existence. The term means, quite simply, that that which is not done by us, is, by definition, undergone.

But this does not in any way prejudge the proportions in which action and passion possess our inner realm. In fact, these two parts of our lives—the active and the passive—are extraordinarily unequal. Seen from our point of view, the active occupies first place because we prefer it and because it is more easily perceived. But in the reality of things the passive is immeasurably the wider and the deeper part.

In the first place the passivities ceaselessly accompany our conscious deeds, in the form of reactions which direct, sustain or oppose our efforts. On this ground alone they inevitably and precisely coincide with the scope of our activities. But their sphere of influence extends far beyond these narrow limits. If we consider the matter carefully we in fact perceive with a sort of dismay that it is only the fine-point of ourselves that emerges into the sphere of reflection and liberty. We know ourselves and set our own course but within an incredibly small radius of light. Immediately beyond lies impenetrable darkness, though it is pregnant with presences—the night of everything that is within us and around us, without us and in spite of us. In this darkness, as vast, rich, troubled and complex as the past and the present of the universe, we are not inert; we react, because we undergo. But this reaction, which operates without our control by an unknown prolongation of our being, is, humanly speaking, still a part of our passivity. In fact, everything beyond a certain distance is dark, and yet everything is full of being around us. This is the darkness, heavy with promises and threats, which the Christian will have to illuminate and animate with the divine Presence.

In the midst of the confused energies which people this restless night, our mere presence immediately brings about the formation of two groups which press in upon us and demand to be treated in very different ways. On one side, the friendly and favourable forces, those which sustain our endeavour and lead us towards achievement—the 'passivities of growth.' On the other side, the hostile powers which laboriously obstruct our tendencies, hamper or deflect our progress towards heightened being, and thwart our real or apparent capacities for development: these are the 'passivities of diminishment.'

Let us look at each group in turn; let us look them in the face until, in the depth of their alluring, unrevealing or hostile gaze, we discern the kindling light of the blessed countenance of God.

2. The Passivities of Growth and the Two Hands of God

Growth seems so natural to us that we do not, as a rule, think of noticing within our action either the forces which nourish it or the circumstances which favour its success. And yet *quid habes quod non accepisti?* (what dost thou possess that thou

hast not previously received?). We undergo life as much as we
undergo death, if not more.

We must try to penetrate our most secret self, and examine
our being from all sides. Let us try, patiently, to perceive the
ocean of forces to which we are subjected and in which our
growth is, as it were, steeped. This is a salutary exercise; for
the depth and universality of our dependence will form the enveloping intimacy of our communion.

. . . And so, for the first time in my life perhaps (although
I am supposed to meditate every day!), I took the lamp and,
leaving the zone of everyday occupations and relationships
where everything seems clear, I went down into my inmost
self, to the deep abyss whence I feel dimly that my power of
action emanates. But as I moved further and further away from
the conventional certainties by which social life is superficially
illuminated, I became aware that I was losing contact with myself. At each step of the descent a new person was disclosed
within me of whose name I was no longer sure, and who no
longer obeyed me. And when I had to stop my exploration because the path faded from beneath my steps, I found a bottom-
less abyss at my feet, and out of it came—arising I know not
from where—the current which I dare to call *my* life.

What science will ever be able to reveal to man the origin,
nature and character of that conscious power to will and to
love which constitutes his life? It is certainly not our effort,
nor the effort of anyone around us, which set that current in
motion. And it is certainly not our solicitude, nor that of any
friend, which prevents its ebb or controls its turbulence. We
can, of course, trace back through generations some of the ante-
cedents of the torrent which bears us along; and we can, by
means of certain moral and physical disciplines and stimula-
tions, regularise or enlarge the aperture through which the torrent is released into us. But neither that geography nor those

artifices help us in theory or in practice to harness the sources of life. My self is given to me far more than it is formed by me. Man, Scripture says, cannot add a cubit to his stature. Still less can he add a unit to the potential of his love, or accelerate by another unit the fundamental rhythm which regulates the ripening of his mind and heart. In the last resort the profound life, the fontal life, the new-born life, escape our grasp entirely.

Stirred by my discovery, I then wanted to return to the light of day and forget the disturbing enigma in the comfortable surroundings of familiar things—to begin living again at the surface without imprudently plumbing the depths of the abyss. But then, beneath this very spectacle of the turmoil of life, there re-appeared, before my newly opened eyes, the unknown that I wanted to escape. This time it was not hiding at the bottom of an abyss; it was concealed beneath the innumerable strands which form the web of chance, the very stuff of which the universe and my own small individuality are woven. Yet it was the same mystery without a doubt: I recognised it. Our mind is perplexed when we try to plumb the depth of the world beneath us. But it reels still more when we try to number the favourable chances which must conjoin at every moment if the least of living things is to survive and to succeed. After the consciousness of being something other and something greater than myself—a second thing made me dizzy: namely, the supreme improbability, the tremendous unlikelihood of finding myself existing in the midst of a world that has survived and succeeded.

At that moment, as anyone else will find who cares to make this same interior experiment, I felt the distress intrinsic to an atom lost in the universe, the distress which makes human wills founder daily under the crushing number of living things and of stars. And if something saved me, it was hearing the voice of the Gospel, guaranteed by divine successes, speaking to me from the depth of the night: *ego sum, noli timere* (It is I, be not afraid).

Yes, O my God, I believe it: and I believe it all the more willingly because it is not only a question of my being consoled, but of my being completed: it is You who are at the origin of the impulse, and at the term of the attraction which I do nothing all my life long but follow, or favour the first impulse and its developments. And it is You who vivify, for me, with Your omnipresence (even more than my spirit vivifies the matter which it animates), the myriad influences of which I am the constant object. In the life which wells up in me and in the matter which sustains me, I find much more than Your gifts. It is You Yourself whom I find, You who make me participate in Your being, You who mould me. It is through the initial control and modulation of the vital force within me, and the favourable and continuous interplay of secondary causes, that I touch, as closely as may be, the two facets of Your creative action; that I encounter, and kiss, Your two marvellous hands— the one which holds us so firmly that it is merged, in us, with the sources of life; and the other whose embrace is so wide that, at its slightest pressure, all the springs of the universe respond harmoniously together. By their very nature, these blessed passivities which are, for me, the will to be, the wish to be thus and thus, and the opportunity to realise myself according to my desire, are all charged with Your influence—an influence which will shortly appear more distinctly to me as the organising energy of the mystical Body. In order to communicate with You in them in a fontal communion (a communion with the sources of Life), I have only to recognise You in them, and to ask You to be ever more present in them.

O God, whose call precedes the very first of our movements, grant me the desire to desire being—that, by means of that di-

vine thirst which is Your gift, the access to the great waters
may open wide within me. Do not deprive me of the sacred
taste for being, that primordial energy, that initial point of support: Spiritu principali confirma me. And You whose loving wisdom forms me out of all the forces and all the hazards of the
earth, grant that I may begin to make a gesture whose full effectiveness I shall feel in the face of the forces of diminishment
and death; grant that, after having desired, I may believe, and
believe ardently and above all things, in Your active Presence.

By Your grace, that expectation and that faith are already
full of operative virtue. But how am I to set about showing You
and proving to myself, through some external effort, that I am
not one of those who say Lord, Lord! with their lips only? I
shall collaborate in Your forestalling action and will do so dou-
bly. First, to Your deep inspiration which commands me to be,
I shall respond by taking great care never to stifle nor distort
nor waste my power to love and to do. Next, to Your all-envel-
oping Providence which shows me at each moment, by the day's
events, the next step to take and the next rung to climb, I shall
respond by my care never to miss an opportunity of rising 'towards the spirit.'

The life of each one of us is, as it were, woven of those two
threads: the thread of inward development, through which our
ideas and affections and our human and mystical attitudes are
gradually formed; and the thread of outward success by which
we always find ourselves at the exact point at which the totality
of the forces of the universe converge to produce upon us the
effect which God desires.

O God, that at all times You may find me as You desire me
and where You would have me be, that You may lay hold on
me fully, both by the Within and the Without of myself, grant
that I may never break this double thread of my life.

3. The Passivities of Diminishment [1]

To cleave to God hidden beneath the inward and outward forces
which animate our being and sustain it in its development, is
ultimately to open ourselves to, and put trust in, all the breaths
of life. We answer to, and 'communicate' with, the passivities
of growth by our fidelity in action. Hence, by our desire to undergo God, we find ourselves brought back to the lovable duty
to grow.

The moment has come to plumb the decidedly negative side
of our existences—the side on which, however far we search, we
cannot discern any happy result or any solid conclusion to what
happens to us. It is easy enough to understand that God can
be grasped in and through every life. But can God also be found
in and through every death? This is what disconcerts us. And
yet this is what we must learn to recognise habitually and in
practice, under pain of remaining blind to what is most specifically Christian in the Christian vision, and under pain, too,
of losing contact with the divine on one of the widest and most
receptive fronts of our life.

[1] If, in speaking of evil in this section, we do not mention sin more
explicitly, it is because the aim of the following pages being solely to
show how all things can help the believer to unite himself to God, there
is no need to concern ourselves directly with bad actions, that is with
positive gestures of disunion. Sin only interests us here in so far as it is
a weakening, a deviation caused by our personal faults (even when re-
pented), or the pain and the scandal which the faults of others inflict
on us. From this point of view it makes us suffer and can be transformed
in the same way as other suffering. That is why physical evil and moral
evil are presented here, almost without distinction, in the same chapter
on the passivities of diminishment.

The forces of diminishment are our real passivities. Their number is vast, their forms infinitely varied, their influence constant. In order to clarify our ideas and direct our meditation we will divide them into two groups corresponding to the two forms under which we considered the forces of growth: the diminishments whose origin lies *within us*, and the diminishments whose origin lies *outside us*.

The external passivities of diminishment are all our bits of ill fortune. We have only to look back on our lives to see them springing up on all sides: the barrier which blocks our way, the wall that hems us in, the stone which throws us from our path, the obstacle that breaks us, the invisible microbe that kills the body, the little word that infects the mind, all the incidents and accidents of varying importance and varying kinds, the tragic interruptions (upsets, shocks, amputations, deaths) which come between the world of 'other' things and the world that radiates out from us. And yet when hail, fire and thieves had taken everything from Job—all his wealth and all his family—Satan could say to God: 'Skin for skin, and all that a man hath he will give for his life. But put forth thy hand, and touch his bone and his flesh: and then thou shalt see that he will bless thee to thy face.' In a sense the loss of things means little to us because we can always imagine getting them back. What is terrible for us is to be cut off from things through some inward and irretrievable diminishment.

Humanly speaking, the internal passivities of diminishment form the blackest residue and the most despairingly useless years of our life. Some were waiting to pounce on us as we first awoke: natural failings, physical defects, intellectual or moral limitations, as a result of which the field of our activities, of our enjoyment, of our vision, has been ruthlessly limited since birth. Others were lying in wait for us later on and appeared as suddenly and brutally as an accident, or as stealthily as an

illness. All of us one day or another will come to realise, if
we have not already done so, that one of these processes of dis-
organisation has installed itself at the very heart of our lives.
Sometimes it is the cells of the body that rebel or become
diseased; at other times the very elements of our personality
seem to be in conflict or to run amok. And then we impotently
stand by and watch collapse, rebellion and inner tyranny, and
no friendly influence can come to our help. And if by chance
we escape, to a greater or lesser extent, the critical forms of
these invasions which appear deep within us and irresistibly
destroy the strength, the light and the love by which we live,
there still remains that slow, essential deterioration which we
cannot escape: old age little by little robbing us of ourselves
and pushing us on towards the end. Time, which postpones
possession, time which tears us away from enjoyment, time
which condemns us all to death—what a formidable passivity is
the passage of time . . .

In death, as in an ocean, all our slow or swift diminishments
flow out and merge. Death is the sum and consummation of all
our diminishments: it is *evil* itself—purely physical evil, in so far
as it results organically from the material plurality in which we
are immersed—but a moral evil too, in so far as this disordered
plurality, the source of all strife and all corruption, is engendered in society or in ourselves by the wrong use of our
liberty.

We must overcome death by finding God in it. And by the
same token, we shall find the divine established in our innermost hearts, in the last stronghold which might have seemed
able to withstand Him.

Here again, as in the case of the 'divinisation' of our human
activities, we shall find the Christian faith absolutely explicit
in its affirmations and practices. Christ has conquered death,
not only by suppressing its evil effects, but by reversing its sting.

By virtue of the Resurrection, nothing any longer kills inevitably but everything is capable of becoming the blessed touch of the divine hands, the blessed influence of the will of God upon our lives. However compromised by our faults, or however cast down by circumstances, our position may be, we can at any moment, by a total redressment, wholly readjust the world around us and take up our lives again in a favourable sense. *Diligentibus Deum omnia convertuntur in bonum.* That is the fact which dominates all explanation and all discussion.

But here again, as in the matter of the saving value of our human endeavour, our mind wants a justification for its hopes in order to surrender itself to them more completely.

Quomodo fiet istud? This study is all the more necessary because the Christian attitude to evil lends itself to some very dangerous misunderstandings. A false interpretation of Christian resignation, together with a false idea of Christian detachment, is the principal source of the antipathies which make a great many Gentiles so sincerely hate the Gospel.

Let us ask ourselves how, and in what circumstances, our apparent deaths, that is to say the waste-matter of our existences, can be integrated into the establishment, around us, of the Kingdom of God and the milieu of God. It will help us to do this if we thoughtfully distinguish two phases, two periods, in the process which culminates in the transfiguration of our diminishments. The first of these phases is that of our struggle against evil. The second is that of defeat and of its transfiguration.

A. *Our struggle with God against evil*

When a Christian suffers, he says 'God has touched me.' The words are pre-eminently true, though their simplicity sums up a whole complex series of operations and it is *only at the end of the series* that we have the right to utter them. For if, in the course of our encounters with evil, we try to distinguish what the Schoolmen term 'the instants of nature,' we shall have, on the contrary, to begin by saying 'God wants to free me from this diminishment—God wants me to help Him to take this chalice from me.' To struggle against evil, and to reduce to a minimum even the ordinary physical evil which threatens us, is unquestionably the first act of our Father who is in heaven; it would be impossible to conceive Him, and still more impossible to love Him, under any other form.

It is a perfectly correct view of things—and strictly consonant with the Gospel—to regard Providence as concerned throughout the ages with the prevention and tending of the wounds of the world. It is in truth God who raises up the great doctors and the great benefactors of the human race in the course of time and in conformity with the general rhythm of progress. It is He who prompts even the most unbelieving to search after all that comforts and all that cures. And surely men recognise the divine Presence instinctively, in the fact that hatreds are appeased and disagreements unravelled in the presence of those who free the body and the mind. Can there be any doubt of it? At the first approach of the diminishments, we cannot hope to find God except by loathing what is coming upon us and doing our best to avoid it. The more we repel suffering at that moment, with our whole heart and our whole strength,[1] the more closely we cleave to the heart and action of God.

---

[1] Without bitterness and without revolt, of course, but with an *anticipatory tendency* to acceptance and final resignation. It is obviously difficult to seperate the two 'instants of nature' without to some extent distorting them in describing them. But there is this to note: the necessity of the initial stage of resistance to evil is clear, and everyone admits it. The failure that follows on laziness, the illness contracted as a result of unjustified imprudence, could not be regarded by anyone as being the *immediate* will of God.

B. Our apparent failure and its transfiguration

With God as our ally we are always certain of saving our souls. But we know too well that there is no guarantee that we shall always avoid suffering or even those inward defeats on account of which we can imagine our lives to be failures. In any event, all of us are growing old and all of us will die. This means to say that, however fine our resistance, at some moment or other we feel the grip of the forces of diminishment, against which we were fighting, gradually gaining mastery over the forces of life, and dragging us, physically vanquished, to the ground. But how can we be defeated if God is fighting on our side? or what does this defeat signify?

The problem of evil, that is to say the reconciling of our failures, even the purely physical ones, with creative goodness and creative power, will always remain one of the most disturbing mysteries of the universe for both our hearts and our minds. A full understanding of the suffering of God's creatures (like that of the pains of the damned) presupposes in us an appreciation of the nature and value of 'participate being' which, for lack of any point of comparison, we cannot have. Yet this much we can see: on the one hand, the work which God has undertaken in uniting Himself intimately to created beings presupposes in them a slow preparation in the course of which they (*who already exist, but are not yet complete*) cannot of their nature avoid the risks (aggravated by an original fault) involved in the imperfect organisation of the multiple principle in them and around them; and on the other hand, because the final victory of good over evil can only be completed in the *total* organisation of the world, our infinitely short individual lives cannot hope to benefit here below from access to the Promised Land. We are like soldiers who fall during the assault which

leads to peace. God does not therefore suffer a preliminary defeat in our defeat because, although we appear to succumb
individually, the world, in which we shall live again, triumphs
in and through our deaths.

But this first aspect of His victory, which is enough to assure
us of His omnipotence, is completed by another manifestation
—possibly more direct and in any case more immediately palpable for each of us—of His universal authority. In virtue of His
very perfections,[1] God cannot ordain that the elements of a
world in the course of growth—or at least of a fallen world in
the process of rising again—should avoid shocks and diminishments, even moral ones: *necessarium est ut scandala eveniant.*
But God will make it good—He will take His revenge, if one
may use the expression—by making evil itself serve the higher
good of His faithful, the very evil which the present state of
creation does not allow Him to suppress immediately. Like an
artist making use of a fault or an impurity in the stone he is
sculpting or the bronze he is casting so as to produce more
exquisite lines or a more beautiful tone, God, without sparing
us the partial deaths, nor the final death, which form an essential part of our lives, transfigures them by integrating them in
a better plan—*provided we trust lovingly in Him.* Not only
our unavoidable ills but our faults, even our most deliberate
ones, can be embraced in that transformation, provided always
we repent of them. Not everything is immediately good to those
who seek God; but everything is capable of becoming good:
omnia convertuntur in bonum.[2]

---

[1] Because His perfections cannot run counter to the nature of things,
and because a world, assumed to be progressing towards perfection, or
'rising upward,' is of its nature precisely still partially disorganised. A
world without a trace or a threat of evil would be a world already consummated.

[2] On the 'miraculous' effects of faith, see p. 115. There is obviously
no intension of giving a general theory of prayer here.

What is the process and what are the phases by which God accomplishes this marvellous transformation of our deaths into a better life? With the help of analogies drawn from our own capacities, and by reflecting on what has always been the attitude and practical teaching of the Church with regard to human suffering, we may perhaps hazard an answer to this question.

It could be said that Providence, for those who believe in it, converts evil into good in three principal ways. Sometimes a failure we have undergone will divert our activity onto objects, or towards a framework, that are more propitious—though still remaining on the plane of the human ends we are pursuing. That is what happened with Job, whose final happiness was greater than his first. At other times, more often perhaps, the loss which afflicts us will oblige us to turn for the satisfaction of our frustrated desires to less material fields, which neither moth nor rust can corrupt. The lives of the saints and, generally speaking, the lives of all those who have been outstanding for intelligence or goodness, are full of these instances in which one can see the man emerging ennobled, tempered and renewed from some ordeal, or even some downfall, which seemed bound to diminish or lay him low for ever. Failure in that case plays for us the part that the elevator plays for an aircraft or the pruning knife for a plant. It canalises the sap of our inward life, disengages the purest 'components' of our being in such a way as to make us shoot up higher and straighter. The collapse, even when a moral one, is thus transformed into a success which, however spiritual it may be is, nevertheless, felt *experimentally*. In the presence of St. Augustine, St. Mary Magdalen or St. Lydwine, no one hesitates to think *felix dolor* or *felix culpa*. With the result that, up to this point, we still 'understand' Providence.

But there are more difficult cases (the most common ones, in fact) which utterly disconcert our wisdom. At every moment

we see diminishment, both in us and around us, which does
not seem to be compensated by advantages on any perceptible
plane: premature deaths, stupid accidents, weaknesses affecting
the highest reaches of our being. Under blows such as these,
man does not move upward in any appreciable direction; he
disappears or remains tragically diminished. How can these un-
compensated diminishments, which are death in its narrowly
mortal form, become a good for us? This is where we can see
the third way in which Providence operates in the domain of
our diminishments—the most efficacious and the most sanctifying way.

God, as we have seen, has already transfigured our sufferings
by making them serve our conscious fulfilment. In His hands
the forces of diminishment have perceptibly become the instrument that cuts, carves and polishes within us the stone which
is destined to occupy a specific place in the heavenly Jerusalem.
But He will do still more for, as a result of His omnipotence
impinging upon our faith, events which show themselves experimentally in our lives as pure loss will become an immediate
factor in the union we dream of establishing with Him.

Uniting oneself means, in every case, migrating, and dying
partially in what one loves. But if, as we are convinced, this
annihilation in the other must be more complete the more
we attach ourselves to something greater than ourselves, then
we cannot set limits to the sacrifice required of us on our jour-
ney to God. The progressive destruction of our egoism by means
of the 'automatic' broadening of our human perspectives (analysed above on p. 41) when linked to the gradual spiritualisation of our desires and ambitions under the action of certain
setbacks, are no doubt very real forms of that ecstasy which is
to tear us from ourselves so as to subordinate us to God. Yet
the effect of this initial detachment is for the moment only
to develop the centre of our personality to its utmost limits.

Arrived at that ultimate point we may still have the impression
of possessing ourselves in a supreme degree—of being freer and
more active than ever. We have not yet crossed the critical
point of our ex-centration, of our reversion to God. There is a
further step to take: the one that makes us *lose all foothold
within ourselves—oportet illum crescere, me autem minui.* We
are still not lost to ourselves. What will be the agent of that
definitive transformation? Nothing else than death.

In itself, death is an incurable weakness of corporeal beings,
complicated, in our world, by the influence of an original fall.
It is the sum and type of all the forces that diminish us, and
against which we must fight without being able to hope for a
personal, direct and immediate victory. Now the great victory
of the Creator and Redeemer, in the Christian vision, is to have
transformed what is in itself a universal power of diminishment
and extinction into an essentially life-giving factor. God must,
in some way or other, make room for Himself, hollowing us
out and emptying us, if He is finally to penetrate into us. And
in order to assimilate us in Him, He must break the molecules
of our being so as to re-cast and re-model us. The function of
death is to provide the necessary entrance into our inmost selves.
It will make us undergo the required dissociation. It will put
us into the state organically needed if the divine fire is to
descend upon us. And in that way its fatal power to decompose
and dissolve will be harnessed to the most sublime operations
of life. What was by nature empty and void, a return to plurality, can, in each human existence, become plenitude and unity
in God.

C. *Communion through diminishment*

*It was a joy to me, O God, in the midst of the struggle, to
feel that in developing myself I was increasing the hold that*

You have upon me; it was a joy to me, too, under the inward pressure of life or amid the favourable play of events, to abandon myself to Your Providence. Now that I have found the joy of utilizing all forms of growth to make You, or to let You, grow in me, grant that I may willingly consent to this last phase of communion in the course of which I shall possess You by diminishing in You.

After having perceived You as: He who is 'a greater myself,' grant, when my hour comes, that I may recognise You under the species of such alien or hostile force that seems bent upon destroying or supplanting me. When the signs of age begin to mark my body (and still more when they touch my mind); when the ill that is to diminish me or carry me off strikes from without or is born within me; when the painful moment comes in which I suddenly awaken to the fact that I am ill or growing old; and above all at that last moment when I feel I am losing hold of myself and am absolutely passive within the hands of the great unknown forces that have formed me; in all those dark moments, O God, grant that I may understand that it is You (provided only my faith is strong enough) who are painfully parting the fibres of my being in order to penetrate to the very marrow of my substance and bear me away within Yourself.

The more deeply and incurably the evil is encrusted in my flesh, the more it will be You that I am harbouring—You as a loving, active principle of purification and detachment. The more the future opens before me like some dizzy abyss or dark tunnel, the more confident I may be—if I venture forward on the strength of Your word—of losing myself and surrendering myself in You, of being assimilated by Your body, Jesus.

You are the irresistible and vivifying force, O Lord, and because Yours is the energy, because, of the two of us, You are infinitely the stronger, it is on You that falls the part of consuming me in the union that should weld us together. Vouch-

safe, therefore, something more precious still than the grace for which all the faithful pray. It is not enough that I should die while communicating. Teach me to communicate while dying.

D. True resignation

The above analysis (in which we have tried to distinguish the phases by which our diminishments may be divinised) has helped us to justify to ourselves the Christian formula, which is so comforting to those who suffer, 'God has touched me. God has taken away from me. His will be done.' As a result of this analysis we have understood how the two hands of God can reappear, more active and more penetrating than ever, beneath the evils that corrupt us from within, and the blows that crush us from without. But the analysis has a further result, almost as priceless as the first. It puts those of us who are Christians in a position to justify to those who are not Christians the legitimacy and the human value of resignation.

There are many reasonable men who honestly consider and denounce Christian resignation as being one of the most dangerous and soporific elements in 'the opiate of the people.' Next to disgust with the earth, there is no attitude which the Gospel is so bitterly reproached with having fostered as that of passivity in the face of evil—a passivity which can go as far as a perverse cultivation of suffering and diminishment. As we have already said, with reference to 'false detachment': this accusation, or even suspicion, is infinitely more effective, at this moment, in preventing the conversion of the world than all the objections drawn from science or philosophy. A religion which is judged to be inferior to our human ideal—in spite of the marvels by which it is surrounded—is already condemned. It is therefore of supreme importance for the Christian to understand and

live submission to the will of God in the *active* sense which, as
we have said, is the only orthodox sense.

No, if he is to practise to the full the perfection of his Christianity, the Christian must not falter in his duty to resist evil.
On the contrary, during the first phase, as we have seen, he
must fight sincerely and with all his strength, in union with
the creative force of the world, to drive back evil—so that nothing in him or around him may be diminished. During this initial
phase, the believer is the convinced ally of all those who think
that humanity will not succeed unless it strives with all its
might to realise its potentialities. And as we said with reference
to human development, the believer is more closely tied than
anyone to this great task, because in his eyes the victory of
humanity over the diminishments of the world—even physical
and natural—to some extent condition the fulfilment and consummation of the quite specific Reality which he adores. As long
as resistance is possible, the son of heaven will resist too—as
firmly as the most worldly children of the world—everything
that deserves to be scattered or destroyed.

Should he meet with defeat—the personal defeat which no
human being can hope to escape in his brief single combat with
forces whose order of magnitude and evolution are universal—
he will, like the conquered pagan hero, still inwardly resist.
Though he is stifled and constrained, his efforts will still be sustained. At that point, however, he will see a new realm of possibilities open out before him, instead of having nothing to
compensate and dominate his coming death except the melan-
choly and questionable consolation of stoicism (which, if carefully analysed, would probably prove in the end to owe its
beauty and consistency to a despairing faith *in the value of
sacrifice*). This hostile force that lays him low and disintegrates
him can become for him a loving principle of renewal, if he

accepts it with faith and never ceases to struggle against it. On the experimental plane, everything is lost. But in the realm of the supernatural, as it is called, *there is a further dimension* which allows God to achieve, *insensibly,* a mysterious reversal of evil into good. Leaving the zone of human successes and failures behind him, the Christian accedes by an effort of trust in the greater than himself to the region of supra-sensible trans-formations and growth. His resignation is no more than the thrust which lifts the field of his activity higher.

We have come a long way, Christianly speaking, from the justly criticised notion of 'submission to the will of God' which is in danger of weakening and softening the fine steel of the human will, brandished against all the powers of darkness and diminishment. We must understand this well, and cause it to be understood: to find and to do the will of God (even as we diminish and as we die) does not imply either a direct en-counter or a passive attitude. I have no right to regard the evil that comes upon me through my own negligence or fault as being the touch of God.[1] I can only unite myself to the will of God (as endured passively) *when all my strength is spent,* at the point where my activity, fully extended and straining to-wards betterment (understood in ordinary human terms), finds itself continually counter-weighted by forces tending to halt me or overwhelm me. Unless I do everything I can to advance or resist, I shall not find myself at the *required point*—I shall not submit to God as much as I might have done or as much as He wishes. If, on the contrary, I persevere courageously, I shall rejoin God across evil, deeper down than evil; I shall draw close to Him; and at that moment the optimum of my

---

[1] Though the harm which results from my negligence can become the will of God for me on condition I repent and correct my lazy or indif-ferent attitude of mind. Everything can be taken up again and re-cast in God, even one's faults.

'communion in resignation' necessarily coincides (by definition) with the maximum of fidelity to the human task.

Editor's Note.

It is interesting to compare these pages on 'the divinisation of the activities and passivities' with the following clarifications taken from a letter written shortly before *The Divine Milieu,* in which the author sets out his spiritual doctrine to Father Auguste Valensin, one of his closest friends.

'I agree, fundamentally, that the completion of the world is only consummated through a death, a "night," a reversal, an ex-centration, and a quasi-depersonalisation . . . Union with Christ presupposes essentially that we transpose the ultimate centre of our existence into Him—which implies the radical sacrifice of Egoism . . .

(Nevertheless)

'If Christ is to take possession of all my life—of all life— then it is essential that I should grow in Him not only by means of the ascetic constraints and the supremely unifying amputations of suffering, but also by means of everything that my existence brings with it of positive effort, and the perfecting of my nature.

'The formula for renunciation, if it is to be total, must satisfy two conditions:

1. It must enable us to go beyond everything there is in the world
2. And yet at the same time compel us to press forward (with conviction and passion) the development of this same world.

'Speaking in general, Christ gives Himself to us through the world which is to be consummated in relation to Him.

'You should note the following point carefully: I do not attribute any definitive or absolute value to the varied constructions of nature. What I like about them is not their particular form, but their function, which is to build up mysteriously, first what can be divinised, and then, through the grace of Christ coming down upon our endeavour, what is divine . . .

'To sum up, *complete* Christian endeavour consists, in my view, in three things:

1. collaborating passionately in the human effort in the conviction that, not only through our fidelity and obedience, but also through the *work* realised, we are working for the fulfilment of the Pleroma by preparing its more or less immediate material

2. in the course of this hard labour, and in the pursuit of an ever widening ideal, achieving a preliminary form of renunciation and of victory over a narrow and lazy egoism

3. cherishing the 'hollownesses' as well as the 'fullnesses' of life—that is to say its passivities and the providential diminishments through which Christ transforms directly and eminently into Himself the elements and the personality which we have tried to develop for Him . . .

'In that way detachment and human endeavour are harmonized. It should be added that the ways in which they can be combined are infinitely varied. There is an infinity of vocations. Within the Church there are St. Thomas Aquinas and St. Vincent de Paul side by side with St. John of the Cross. There is a time for growth and a time for diminishment in the lives of each one of us. At one moment the dominant note is one of constructive human effort, and at another mystical annihilation . . .

'All these attitudes spring from the same inner orientation of the mind, from a single law which combines the two-fold movement of the natural personalisation of man and his supernatural depersonalisation *in Christo* . . .'

SOME GENERAL REMARKS ON
CHRISTIAN ASCETICISM

Having observed the progressive invasion of divinisation into the active and passive halves of our lives, we are now in a position to take a general view of the celestial layers into which this tide of light has plunged us. That will form the third part of this work.

But before setting ourselves to contemplate the divine milieu, we must, for the sake of clarity, sum up in general terms the ascetic doctrine running through the preceding pages.

We shall do this in three sections under the following headings: 1. Attachment and Detachment; 2. The Meaning of the Cross; 3. The Spiritual Power of Matter.

1. Attachment and Detachment

Nemo dat quod non habet. No sweet-smelling smoke without incense. No sacrifice without a victim. How would man give himself to God if he did not exist? What possession could he transfigure by his detachment if his hands were empty?

These common-sense observations enable us to solve, in principle, the question which is often formulated none too well in the following terms: 'Which is better for a Christian: activity or passivity? Life or death? Growth or diminishment? Development or curtailment? Possession or renunciation?'

The general answer to this is: 'Why separate and contrast the two natural phases of a single effort? Your essential duty and desire is to be united with God. But in order to be united, you must first of all *be*—be yourself as completely as possible. And so you must develop yourself and take possession of the world *in order to be*. Once this has been accomplished, then is the time to think about renunciation; then is the time to accept diminishment for the sake of *being in another*. Such is the sole and two-fold precept of complete Christian asceticism.'

Let us consider the two terms of this method more closely, and observe their particular interplay and the resulting effect.

A. *First, develop yourself,*[1] *Christianity says to the Christian*

Books about the spiritual life do not as a general rule throw this first phase of Christian perfection into relief. Perhaps it seems too obvious to deserve mention, or seems to belong too completely to the 'natural' sphere, or possibly it is too dangerous

---

[1] 'First,' in this sense, clearly indicates a priority in nature as much as, or more than, a priority in time. The true Christian should obviously never be *purely and simply* attached to whatever it may be, because the contact he seeks with things is always made *with a view to* transcending them or transfiguring them. So that when we speak here of being attached, we mean something penetrated and dominated by detachment. (See below in the text).

Nevertheless, the use and proportion of *development* in the spiritual life are very delicate matters, for nothing is easier than to pursue one's selfish interests under cover of growing and of loving in God. The only real protection against that dangerous illusion is a constant concern to keep very much alive (with God's help) the impassioned vision of the *Greater than All*. In the presence of that supreme interest, the very idea of growing or enjoying egotistically, for oneself, becomes insipid and intolerable.

to be insisted upon—whatever the reason, these books usually remain silent on the subject or take it for granted. This is a fault and an omission. Although the majority of people understand it easily enough, and although its essentials are common to the ethics of both layman and religious, the duty of human perfection, like the whole universe, has been renewed, recast, supernaturalised, in the Kingdom of God. It is a truly Christian duty to grow, even in the eyes of men, and to make one's talents bear fruit, even though they be natural. It is part of the essentially Catholic vision to look upon the world as maturing—not only in each individual or in each nation, but in the whole human race—a specific power of knowing and loving whose transfigured term is charity, but whose roots and elemental sap lie in the discovery and delectation of everything that is true and beautiful in creation. This has already been explained with reference to the Christian value of action; but here is the place to recall it: the effort of mankind, even in realms inaccurately called profane, must, in the Christian life, assume the role of a holy and unifying operation. It is the collaboration, trembling with love, which we give to the hands of God, concerned to attire and prepare us (and the world) for the final union through sacrifice. Understood in this way, the care which we devote to personal achievement and embellishment is no more than a gift begun. And that is why the attachment to creatures which it appears to denote melts imperceptibly into complete detachment.

B. And if you possess something, Christ says in the Gospel, leave it and follow me

Up to a certain point the believer who, understanding the Christian meaning of development, has worked to mould himself and the world for God, will hardly need to hear the second injunction before beginning to obey it. Anyone whose aim, in conquering the earth, has really been to subject a little more matter to spirit has, surely, begun to take leave of himself at the same time as taking possession of himself. This is also true of the man who rejects mere enjoyment, the line of least resistance, the easy possession of things and ideas, and sets out courageously on the path of work, inward renewal and the ceaseless broadening and purification of his ideal. And it is true, again, of the man who has given his time, his health, or his life to something greater than himself—a family to be supported, a country to be saved, a truth to be discovered, a cause to be defended. All these men are continually passing from attachment to detachment as they faithfully mount the ladder of human endeavour.

There are, however, two forms of renunciation which are reserved, and the Christian will not embark upon them except at the invitation or on the express order of his Creator. We refer to the practice of the evangelical counsels, and the use of diminishments, neither of which is justified by the pursuit of a clearly defined higher good.

Where the first are concerned, no one will deny that the religious life (which was also discovered, and is still practised, outside Christianity) can be a normal and 'natural' flowering of human activity in search of a higher life. Nevertheless the practice of the virtues of poverty, chastity and obedience does represent the beginnings of a flight beyond the normal spheres of earthly, procreative and conquering humanity; and for this reason they had to wait, before becoming generally valid and licit, for a *Duc in Altum* to authenticate the aspirations maturing in the human soul. That authorisation was given once and for all in the Gospel by the Master of things. But it must also be heard individually by those who are to benefit from it: it is 'vocation.'

With the practice of the forces of diminishment, the initiative must, even more clearly, come entirely from God. Man can and should make use of penances of some kind to organise the hierarchy of, and liberate, the lower forces within him. He can and should sacrifice himself when a greater interest claims him. But he has not the right to diminish himself for the sake of diminishing himself. Voluntary mutilation, even when conceived as a method of inward liberation, is a crime against being, and Christianity has always explicitly condemned it. The Church's most firmly established teaching is that it is our duty as creatures to try and live more and more by the higher parts of ourselves, in conformity with the aspirations of the present life. That alone is our concern. The rest belongs to the wisdom of Him who alone can bring forth another life from every form of death.

There is no need to be wildly impatient. The Master of death will come soon enough—and perhaps we can already hear His footsteps. There is no need to forestall His hour nor to fear it. When He enters into us to destroy, as it seems, the virtues and the forces that we have distilled with so much loving care out of the sap of the world, it will be as a loving fire to consummate our completion in union.

C. Thus, in the general rhythm of Christian life, development and renunciation, attachment and detachment, are not mutually exclusive

On the contrary, they harmonise, like breathing in and out in the movement of our lungs. They are two phases of the soul's breath, or two components of the impulse by which the Christian life uses things as a springboard from which to transcend them.[1]

That is the general solution. In the detail of particular cases, the sequence of these two phases and the combinations of these two components are subject to an infinite number of subtle variations. Their exact blending calls for a spiritual tact which is the strength and virtue proper to the masters of the inner life. In some Christians detachment will always retain the form of disinterestedness and endeavour, which belongs to human work faithfully carried out: the transfiguration of life will be wholly inward. In others a physical or moral caesura will occur in the course of their lives which will cause them to pass from the level of a very holy normal life to the level of elected renunciations and mystical states. But for all of them, in any event, the road ends at the same point: the final stripping in death which accompanies the recasting, and is a prelude to the final incorporation, *in Christo Jesu*. And for all of them again, what makes or mars their life is the degree of harmony with which the two factors of growing for Christ, and diminishing in Him, are combined in the light of the natural and supernatural aptitudes involved. It would clearly be as absurd to prescribe unlimited development or renunciation as it would be to set no bounds to eating or fasting. In the spiritual life, as in all organic

---

[1] From this 'dynamic' point of view the opposition so often stressed between asceticism and mysticism disappears. There is nothing in man's concern for self-perfection to distract him from his absorption in God, provided the ascetic effort is simply the beginning of 'mystical annihilation.' There is no longer any reason to distinguish between an (ascetic) 'anthropomorphism' and a (mystical) 'theocentrism,' once the human centre is seen and loved in conjunction with (that is, in movement towards) the divine centre. Of course as God takes possession of man, the creature finally becomes passive (because it finds itself newly created in the divine union). But that passivity presupposes a subject that reacts and an active phase. The fire of heaven must come down on something: otherwise there would be nothing consumed and nothing consummated.

processes, everyone has his *optimum* and it is just as harmful to go beyond it as not to attain it.[1]

What has been said of individuals must be transposed and applied to the Church as a whole. It is probable that the Church is led, at different times in the course of her existence, to emphasise in her general life now a greater care to collaborate in the earthly task, now a more jealous concern to stress the ultimate transcendence of her preoccupations. What is quite certain is that her health and integrity, at any given moment, depend upon the exactitude with which her members, each in their proper place, fulfil their functions which range from the duty of applying themselves to what are reputed to be the most profane of worldly occupations, to vocations which call for the most austere penances or the most sublime contemplation. All those different roles are necessary. The Church is like a great tree whose roots must be energetically anchored in the earth while its leaves are serenely exposed to the bright sunlight. In this way she sums up a whole gamut of pulsations in a single vital and synthetic act, each one of which corresponds to a particular degree or a possible form of spiritualisation.

In the midst of all that diversity there is, however, something

---

[1] One thus evades the basic problem of the use of creatures if one solves it by saying that in all cases the *least possible* should be taken from them. This *minimum* theory is no doubt the product of the mistaken notion that God grows in us by destruction or substitution rather than by transformation (see note p. 86) or, which comes to the same thing, that the spiritual potential of the material creation is now exhausted. The *minimum* theory may be useful in reducing certain seeming risks; it does not teach us how to get the maximum spiritual yield from the objects which surround us—which is what the reign of God really means. The one absolute rule upon which we can depend in this matter would seem to be this: 'To love in the world, in God, something which may always become greater.' All the rest is a matter of Christian prudence and individual vocation. See pp. 82-84 on the utilisation by each of us of the spiritual forces in matter.

which dominates—something which confers its distinctive Christian character on the organism as a whole (as well as upon each element in it): it is the impulse towards the heavens, the laborious and painful ecstasy piercing through matter. It is important to remember (and we have not finished insisting on it) that the supernatural awaits and sustains the progress of our nature. But it must not be forgotten that it purifies and perfects that progress, in the end, only in an apparent annihilation. The inseparable alliance between the two terms, personal progress and renunciation in God; but also the continual, and then final, ascendency of the second over the first—it is these that sum up the full meaning of the mystery of the Cross.

2. The Meaning of the Cross

The Cross has always been a symbol of conflict, and a principle of selection, among men. The Faith tells us that it is by the willed attraction or repulsion exercised upon souls by the Cross that the sorting of the good seed from the bad, the separation of the chosen elements from the unutilisable ones, is accomplished at the heart of mankind. Wherever the Cross appears, unrest and antagonisms are inevitable. But there is no reason why these conflicts should be needlessly exacerbated by preaching the doctrine of Christ crucified in a discordant or provocative manner. Far too often the Cross is presented for our adoration, not so much as a sublime end to be attained by our transcending ourselves, but as a symbol of sadness, of limitation and repression.

This way of preaching the Passion is, in many cases, merely the result of the inept use of pious vocabulary in which the most solemn words (sacrifice, immolation, expiation), devoided of their meaning by routine, are used, quite unconsciously, in a light and frivolous way. They become formulas to be juggled with. But this manner of speech ends by conveying the impression that the Kingdom of God can only be established in mourning, and by thwarting and going against the current of man's aspirations and energies. By words that are, in themselves, faithful to their meaning, a picture is revealed than which nothing could really be less Christian. What we said just now about the necessary combination of attachment and detachment allows of giving Christian asceticism a much richer and a far more complete meaning.

In its highest and most general sense, the doctrine of the Cross is that to which all men adhere who believe that the vast movement and agitation of human life opens on to a road which leads somewhere, and that that road *climbs upward*. Life has a term: therefore it imposes a particular direction, oriented, in fact, towards the highest possible spiritualisation by means of the greatest possible effort. To admit that group of fundamental principles is already to range oneself among the disciples—distant, perhaps, and implicit, but nevertheless real—of Christ Crucified. Once that first choice has been made, the first distinction has been drawn between the brave who will succeed and the pleasure-seekers who will fail, between the elect and the condemned.

This rather vague attitude is clarified and carried further by Christianity. Above all, by revealing an original fall, Christianity provides our intelligence with a reason for the disconcerting excess of sin and suffering at certain points. Next, in order to win our love and secure our faith, it unveils to our eyes and hearts the moving and unfathomable reality of the historical Christ in whom the exemplary life of an individual man conceals this mysterious drama: the Master of the world, leading, like an element of the world, not only an elemental life, but (in addition to this and because of it) leading the total life of the universe, which He has shouldered and assimilated by experiencing it Himself. And finally, by the crucifixion and death of this adored Being, Christianity signifies to our thirst for happiness that the term of creation is not to be sought in the temporal zones of our visible world, but that the effort required of our fidelity must be consummated *beyond a total metamorphosis* of ourselves and of everything surrounding us.

Thus the perspectives of renunciation implied in the exercise of life itself are gradually expanded. Ultimately we find ourselves thoroughly uprooted, as the Gospel desires, from everything tangible on earth. But the process of uprooting ourselves has happened little by little and according to a rhythm which has neither alarmed nor wounded the respect we owe to the admirable beauties of the human effort.

It is perfectly true that the Cross means going beyond the frontiers of the sensible world and even, in a sense, breaking with it. The final stages of the ascent to which it calls us compel us to cross a threshold, a critical point, where we lose touch with the zone of the realities of the senses. That final 'excess,' glimpsed and accepted from the first steps, inevitably puts everything we do in a special light and gives it a particular significance. That is exactly where the folly of Christianity lies in the eyes of the 'wise' who are not prepared to stake the good which they now hold in their hands on a total 'Beyond.' But that agonising flight from the experimental zones—which is what the Cross means—is only (as should be strongly emphasised) the sublime aspect of a law common to *all* life. Towards the summit, wrapped in mist to our human eyes and to which the Cross invites us, we rise by a path which is the way of universal progress. The royal road of the Cross is no more nor less than the road of human endeavour supernaturally righted and prolonged. Once we have fully grasped the meaning of the

Cross, we are no longer in danger of finding life sad and ugly. We shall simply have become more attentive to its incomprehensible gravity.

To sum up, Jesus on the Cross is both the symbol and the reality of the immense labour of the centuries which has, little by little, raised up the created spirit and brought it back to the depths of the divine context. He represents (and in a true sense, He is) creation, as, sustained by God, it re-ascends the slopes of being, sometimes clinging to things for support, sometimes tearing itself from them in order to transcend them, and always compensating, by physical suffering, for the setbacks caused by its moral downfalls.

The Cross is therefore not inhuman but superhuman. We can now understand that from the very first, from the very origins of mankind as we know it, the Cross was placed on the crest of the road which leads to the highest peaks of creation. But, in the growing light of revelation, its arms, which at first were bare, show themselves to have put on Christ: *Crux inuncta.* At first sight the bleeding body may seem mournful to us. Is it not from the night that it shines forth? But if we go nearer we shall recognise the flaming Seraphim of Alvernus whose passion and compassion are *incendium mentis.* The Christian is not asked to swoon in the shadow, but to climb in the light, of the Cross.

Editor's Note.

In pages that were not, like *The Divine Milieu,* intended for 'the waverers, both inside and outside,' Father Teilhard, in the course of a meditation, freely expressed the capital importance which he attached to the priestly and religious vocation, to the evangelical counsels, and to the redemptive power

of death. The following short extracts will give an idea of the
substance of his convictions:

'Every priest, because he is a priest, has dedicated his
life to the work of universal salvation. If he is conscious of
the dignity of his office, he should no longer live for himself but for the world, following the example of Him whom
he is anointed to represent.

'To the full extent of my power, *because I am a priest*,
I wish from now on to be the first to become conscious
of all that the world loves, pursues and suffers; I want to
be the first to seek, to sympathise and to suffer; the first
to unfold and sacrifice myself—to become more widely human and more nobly of the earth than any of the world's
servants . . .

'At the same time, by the practice of the counsels, and
through renunciation, I want to recover all that there may
be of heavenly fire in the three-fold concupiscence—I want
to sanctify, through chastity, poverty and obedience, the
power invested in love, in gold and in independence.

'Was there ever a humanity, O Lord, more like, in its
blood, an immolated victim; more adapted, by its inward
unrest, to creative transformations; more rich, with its vio-
lence, in sanctifiable energy; more close, in its anguish, to
supreme communion? . . .

'O Priests! Never have you been priests in so full a
sense as now, merged and submerged as you are in the pains
and the blood of a generation—never so active, never so
directly on the path of your vocation . . .

'I feel so weak, Lord, that I hardly dare ask you to let
me participate in that beatitude. But I perceive it clearly
enough, and I proclaim it:

'Happy are those of us who, in these decisive days of
the Creation and the Redemption, are chosen for this su-

preme act, the logical crowning of their priesthood: communion unto death with Christ . . .'

(from *Le Prêtre.*)

3. *The Spiritual Power of Matter*

The same beam of light which Christian spirituality, rightly and fully understood, directs upon the Cross to humanise it (without veiling it) is reflected on matter so as to spiritualise it.

In their struggle towards the mystical life, men have often succumbed to the illusion of crudely contrasting soul and body, spirit and flesh, as though they were good and evil. But despite certain current expressions, this Manichean tendency has never had the Church's approval. And, in order to prepare the way for our final view of the divine milieu, perhaps we may be allowed to vindicate and exalt that aspect of it which the Lord came to put on, save and consecrate: *holy matter.*

From the mystical and ascetic point of view adopted in these pages, matter is not exactly any of the abstract entities defined under that name by science and philosophy. It is certainly the same *concrete* reality, for us, as it is for physics and metaphysics, having the same basic attributes of plurality, tangibility and inter-connection. But here we want to embrace that reality as a whole in its widest possible sense: to give it its full abundance as it reacts not only to our scientific or dialectical investigations, but to all our practical activities. Matter, as far as we are concerned, is the assemblage of things, energies and creatures which surround us in so far as these are palpable, sensible and 'natural' (in the theological sense of the word). Matter is the common, universal, tangible setting, infinitely shifting and varied, in which we live.

How, then, does the thing thus defined present itself to us
to be acted upon? Under the enigmatic features of a two-sided
power.

On the one hand matter is the burden, the chain, the pain,
the sin and the threat to our lives. It weighs us down, suffers,
wounds, tempts and grows old. Matter makes us heavy, paralysed, vulnerable, guilty. Who will deliver us from this body
of death?

But at the same time matter is physical exuberance, en-
nobling contact, virile effort and the joy of growth. It attracts,
renews, unites and flowers. By matter we are nourished, lifted
up, linked to everything else, invaded by life. To be deprived
of it is intolerable. *Non exui volumus sed superindui* (2 Cor.
v, 4). Who will give us an immortal body?

Asceticism deliberately looks no further than the first aspect,
the one which is turned towards death; and it recoils, exclaim-
ing 'Flee!' *But what would our spirits be, O God, if they did
not have the bread of earthly things to nourish them, the wine
of created beauties to intoxicate them, and the conflicts of
human life to fortify them? What feeble powers and bloodless
hearts Your creatures would bring You if they were to succeed
in cutting themselves off prematurely from the providential setting in which You have placed them! Teach us, Lord, how to
contemplate the sphinx without succumbing to its spell; how
to grasp the mystery hidden in the womb of death not by a
refinement of human doctrine, but in the simple concrete act
by which You immersed Yourself in matter in order to redeem
it. By the virtue of Your suffering Incarnation disclose to us,
and then teach us to harness jealously for You, the spiritual
power of matter.*

Let us take a comparison as our starting point. Imagine a
deep-sea diver trying to get back from the seabed to the clear
light of day. Or imagine a traveller on a fog-bound mountain-

side climbing upward towards the summit bathed in light. For each of these men space is divided into two zones marked with opposing properties: the one behind and beneath appears ever darker, while the one in front and above becomes ever lighter. Both diver and climber can succeed in making their way towards the second zone only if they use everything around and about them as points of leverage. Moreover, in the course of their task, the light above them grows brighter with each advance made; and at the same time the area which has been traversed, as it is traversed, ceases to hold the light and is engulfed in darkness. Let us remember these stages, for they express symbolically all the elements we need in order to understand how we should touch and handle matter with a proper sense of reverence.

Above all, matter is not just the weight that drags us down, the mire that sucks us in, the bramble that bars our way. In itself, and anterior to our position and our choice, it is simply the slope on which we can go up just as well as go down, the medium that can uphold just as well as give way, the wind that can overthrow or lift up. Of its nature, and as a result of original sin, it is true that it represents a perpetual aspiration towards failure. But by nature too, and as a result of the Incarnation, it contains the spur or the allurement to be our accomplice towards heightened being, and this counterbalances and even dominates the *fomes peccati*. The full truth of our situation is that, here below, and by virtue of our immersion in the universe, we are each one of us placed within its layers, or on its slopes, at a specific point defined by the present moment in the history of the world, the locality of our birth, and our individual vocation. And *from that starting point*, variously situated at different levels, the task assigned to us is to climb towards the light, passing through, so as to attain God, *a given series of created things* which are not exactly obstacles but rather foot-holds, intermediaries to be made use of, nourishment to be taken, sap to be purified, and elements to be associated with us and borne along with us.

That being so, and still as a result of our initial position among things, and also as a result of each position we subsequently occupy in matter, matter falls into two distinct zones, differentiated according to our effort: the zone already left behind or arrived at, to which we should not return, or at which we should not pause, lest we fall back—this is the zone of matter *in the material and carnal sense*; and the zone offered to our renewed efforts towards progress, search, conquest and 'divinisation,' the zone of matter *taken in the spiritual sense*; and the frontier between these two zones is essentially relative and shifting. That which is good, sanctifying and spiritual for my brother below or beside me on the mountainside, can be material, misleading or bad for me. What I rightly allowed myself yesterday, I must perhaps deny myself today. And conversely, actions which would have been a grave betrayal in a St. Louis of Gonzaga or a St. Anthony, may well be models for me if I am to follow in the footsteps of these saints. In other words, the soul can only rejoin God after having traversed *a specific path* through matter—which path can be seen as the distance which separates, but it can also be seen as the road which links. Without certain possessions and certain victories, no man exists as God wishes him to be. Each one of us has his Jacob's ladder, whose rungs are formed of a series of objects. Thus it is not our business to withdraw from the world before our time; rather let us learn to orient our being in the flux of things; then, instead of the force of gravity which drags us down to the abyss of self-indulgence and selfishness, we shall feel a salutary 'component' emerge from created things which by a process we have already described will augment us, will snatch us away from our pettinesses and impel us imperiously towards a widening of our vision, towards the renunciation of cherished pleasures, towards the desire for ever more spiritual beauty. Matter, which at first seemed to counsel us towards the maximum pleasure and the minimum effort, emerges as the principle of minimum pleasure and maximum effort.

In this case, too, the law which applies to the individual would seem to be a small-scale version of the law which applies to the whole. It would surely not be far wrong to suggest that, in its universality, the world too has a prescribed path to follow before attaining its consummation. There can really be no doubt of it. If the material totality of the world includes energies which cannot be made use of, and if, more unfortunately, it contains perverted energies and elements which are slowly separated from it, it is still more certain that it contains *a certain quantity of spiritual power* of which the progressive sublimation, *in Christo Jesu*, is, for the Creator, the fundamental operation taking place. At the present time this power is still diffused almost everywhere: nothing, however insignificant or crude it may appear, is without some trace of it. And the task of the Body of Christ, living in His faithful, is patiently to sort out those celestial forces—to extract, without letting any of it be lost, that chosen substance. Little by little, we may rest assured, the work is being done. Thanks to the multitude of individuals and vocations, the Spirit of God insinuates itself everywhere and is everywhere at work. It is the great tree we spoke of a moment ago, whose sunlit branches refine and turn to flowers the sap extracted by the humblest of its roots. As the work progresses, certain zones, no doubt, become worked out. Within each individual life, as we have noted, the frontier between spiritual matter and carnal matter is constantly moving upward. And in the same way, in proportion as humanity is Christianised, it feels less and less need for certain earthly nourishment. Contemplation and chastity should thus tend, quite legitimately, to gain mastery over anxious work and direct possession. This is the general 'drift' of matter towards spirit. This movement must have its term: one day the whole divinisable substance of matter will have passed into the souls of men; all the chosen dynamisms will have been recuperated: and then our world will be ready for the Parousia.

Who can fail to perceive the great symbolic gesture of baptism in this general history of matter? Christ immerses Himself in the waters of Jordan, symbol of the forces of the earth. These He sanctifies. And as He emerges, in the words of St. Gregory of Nyssa, with the water which runs off His body He elevates the whole world.

Immersion and emergence; participation in things and sublimation; possession and renunciation, crossing through and being borne onwards—that is the two-fold yet single movement which answers the challenge of matter in order to save it.[1]

---

[1] The sensual mysticisms and certain neo-pelagianisms (such as "Americanism"), by paying too much attention to the first of these phases, have fallen into the error of seeking divine love and the divine Kingdom *on the same level* as human affections and human progress. Conversely, by concentrating too much on the second phase, some exaggerated forms of Christianity conceive perfection as built upon the destruction of 'nature.' The true Christian supernatural, frequently defined by the Church, neither leaves the creature where he is, on his own plane, nor suppresses him: it 'sur-animates' him. It must surely be obvious that, however transcendent and creative they may be, God's love and ardour could only fall upon the *human* heart, that is to say upon an object prepared (from near or from afar) by means of all the nourishments of the earth. It is astonishing that so few minds should succeed, in this as in other cases, in grasping the notion of transformation. Sometimes the thing transformed seems to them to be the old thing unchanged; at other times they see in it only the entirely new. In the first case it is the spirit that eludes them; in the second case, it is the matter. Though not so crude as the first excess, the second is shown by experience to be no less destructive of the equilibrium of mankind.

Matter, you in whom I find both seduction and strength, you in whom I find blandishment and virility, you who can enrich and destroy, I surrender myself to your mighty layers, with faith in the heavenly influences which have sweetened and purified your waters. The virtue of Christ has passed into you. *Let your attractions lead me forward, let your sap be the food that nourishes me; let your resistance give me toughness; let your robberies and inroads give me freedom. And finally let your whole being lead me towards Godhead.*

PART THREE

THE DIVINE MILIEU

Nemo sibi vivit, aut sibi moritur . . . *Sive vivimus, sive morimur, Christi sumus.*

No man lives or dies to himself. But whether through our life or through our death we belong to Christ.

The first two parts of this Essay are simply an analysis and verification of the above words of St. Paul. We have considered, in turn, the sphere of activity, development and life, and the sphere of passivity, diminishment and death in our lives. All around us, to right and left, in front and behind, above and below, we have only had to go a little beyond the frontier of sensible appearances in order to see the divine welling up and showing through. But it is not only close to us, in front of us, that the divine Presence has revealed itself. It has sprung up so universally, and we find ourselves so surrounded and transfixed by it, that there is no room left to fall down and adore it, even within ourselves.

By means of all created things, without exception, the divine assails us, penetrates us and moulds us. We imagined it as distant and inaccessible, whereas in fact we live steeped in its burning layers. *In eo vivimus.* As Jacob said, awakening from his dream, the world, this palpable world, to which we brought the boredom and callousness reserved for profane places, is in truth a holy place, and we did not know it. *Venite, adoremus.*

Let us withdraw to the higher and more spiritual ether which
bathes us in living light. And let us take joy in making an
inventory of its attributes and recognising their nature, before
examining in a general way the means by which we can open
ourselves ever more to its penetration.

1. The Attributes of the Divine Milieu

The essential marvel of the divine milieu is the ease with which
it assembles and harmonises within itself qualities which appear
to us to be contradictory.

As vast as the world and much more formidable than the
most immense energies of the universe, it nevertheless possesses
in a supreme degree the concentration and the specific qualities which are the charm and warmth of human persons.

Vast and innumerable as the dazzling surge of creatures that
are sustained and sur-animated by its ocean, it nevertheless
retains the concrete transcendence that allows it to bring back
the elements of the world, without the least confusion, within
its triumphant and personal unity.

Incomparably near and tangible—for it presses in upon us
through all the forces of the universe—it nevertheless eludes our
grasp so constantly that we can never seize it here below except
by raising ourselves, uplifted on its waves, to the extreme limit
of our efforts: present in, and drawing at the inaccessible depth
of, each creature, it withdraws always further, bearing us along
with it towards the common centre of all consummation.[1]

---

[1] I attain God in those whom I love to the same degree in which we,
myself and they become more and more spiritual. In the same way,
I grasp Him in the Beautiful and the Good in proportion as I pursue
these further and further with progressively purified faculties.

Through it, the touch of matter is a purification, and chastity flowers as the sublimation of love.

In it, development culminates in renunciation; attachment to things separates us from everything disintegrating in them. Death becomes a resurrection.

Now, if we try to discover the source of so many astonishingly coupled perfections, we shall find they all spring from the same 'fontal' property which we can express thus: God reveals Himself everywhere, beneath our groping efforts, *as a universal milieu*, only because he is *the ultimate point* upon which all realities converge. Each element of the world, whatever it may be, only subsists, *hic et nunc*, in the manner of a cone whose generatrices meet in God who draws them together—(meeting at the term of their individual perfection and at the term of the general perfection of the world which contains them). It follows that all created things, every one of them, cannot be looked at, in their nature and action, without the same reality being found in their innermost being—like sunlight in the fragments of a broken mirror—one beneath its multiplicity, unattainable beneath its proximity, and spiritual beneath its materiality. No object can influence us by its essence without our being touched by the radiance of the focus of the universe. Our minds are incapable of grasping a reality, our hearts and hands of seizing the essentially desirable in it, without our being compelled *by the very structure of things* to go back to the first source of its perfections. This focus, this source, are thus everywhere. It is *precisely because* he is so infinitely profound and punctiform that God is infinitely near, and dispersed everywhere. It is *precisely because* He is the centre that He fills the whole sphere. The omnipresence of the divine is simply the effect of its extreme spirituality and is the exact contrary of the fallacious ubiquity which matter seems to derive from its extreme dissociation and dispersal. In the light of this discovery, we can resume our march through the inexhaustible wonders which the divine milieu has in store for us.

However vast the divine milieu may be, it is in reality a *centre*. It therefore has the properties of a centre, and above all the absolute and final power to unite (and consequently to complete) all beings within its breast. In the divine-milieu all the elements of the universe *touch each other* by that which is most inward and ultimate in them. There they concentrate, little by little, all that is purest and most attractive in them without loss and without danger of subsequent corruption. There they shed, in their meeting, the mutual exteriority and the incoherences which form the basic pain of human relationships. Let those seek refuge there who are saddened by the separations, the parsimonies and the prodigalities of the world. In the external spheres of the world, man is always torn by the separations which set distance between bodies, which set the impossibility of mutual understanding between souls, which set death between lives. Moreover at every minute he must lament that he cannot pursue and embrace everything within the compass of a few years. Finally, and not without reason, he is incessantly distressed by the crazy indifference or the heart-breaking muteness of a natural milieu in which the greater part of individual endeavour seems wasted or lost, where the blow and the cry seem stifled on the spot, without awakening any echo.

All that is only surface desolation.

But let us leave the surface, and, without leaving the world, plunge into God. There, and from there, in Him and through Him, we shall hold all things and have command of all things. There we shall one day rediscover the essence and brilliance of all the flowers and lights which we were forced to abandon so as to be faithful to life. The things we despaired of reaching and influencing are all there, all reunited by the most vulnerable, receptive and enriching point in their substance. In this place the least of our desires and efforts is harvested and tended and can at any moment cause the marrow of the universe to vibrate.

Let us establish ourselves in the divine milieu. There we shall find ourselves where the soul is most deep and where matter is most dense. There we shall discover, with the confluence of all beauties, the ultra-vital, the ultra-sensitive, the ultra-active point of the universe. And, at the same time, we shall feel the *plenitude* of our powers of action and adoration effortlessly ordered within our deepest selves.

But the fact that all the external springs of the world should be co-ordinated and harmonised at that privileged point is not the only marvel. By a complementary marvel, the man who abandons himself to the divine milieu feels his inward powers clearly directed and vastly expanded by it with a sureness which enables him to avoid, like child's play, the reefs on which mystical ardour has so often foundered.

In the first place, the sojourner in the divine milieu is not a pantheist. At first sight, perhaps, the depths of the divine which St. Paul reveals to us may seem to resemble the fascinating domains unfolded before our eyes by monistic philosophies or religions. In fact they are very different, far more reassuring to our minds, far more comforting to our hearts. Pantheism seduces us by its vistas of perfect universal union. But ultimately, if it were true, it would give us only fusion and unconsciousness; for, at the end of the evolution it claims to reveal, the elements of the world vanish in the God they create or by which they are absorbed. Our God, on the contrary, pushes to its furthest possible limit the differentiation among the creatures He concentrates within Himself. At the peak of their adherence to Him, the elect also discover in Him the consummation of their individual fulfilment. Christianity alone therefore saves, with the rights of thought, the essential aspiration of all mysticism: *to be united* (that is, to become the other) *while remaining oneself.* More attractive than any world-Gods, whose eternal seduction it embraces, transcends, and purifies—*in omnibus omnia Deus* (*En pasi panta Theos*)—our divine milieu is at the antipodes of false pantheism. The Christian can plunge himself into it whole-heartedly without the risk of finding himself one day a monist.

Nor is there any reason to fear that in abandoning himself to those deep waters, he will lose his foothold in revelation and in life, and become either unrealistic in the object of his cult or else chimerical in the substance of his work. The Christian lost within the divine layers will not find his mind subject to the forbidden distortions that go to make the 'modernist' or the 'illuminati.'

To the Christian's sensitised vision, it is true, the Creator and, more specifically, the Redeemer (as we shall see) have steeped themselves in all things and penetrated all things to such a degree that, as Blessed Angela of Foligno said, 'the world is full of God.' But this aggrandisement is only valuable in his eyes in so far as the light, in which everything seems to him bathed, radiates from *an historical centre* and is transmitted along *a traditional and solidly defined axis.* The immense enchantment of the divine milieu owes all its value in the long run to the human-divine contact which was revealed at the Epiphany of Jesus. If you suppress the historical reality of Christ, the divine omnipresence which intoxicates us becomes, like all the other dreams of metaphysics, uncertain, vague, conventional—lacking the decisive experimental verification by which to impose itself on our minds, and without the moral directives to assimilate our lives into it. Thenceforward, however dazzling the expansions which we shall try in a moment to discern in the resurrected Christ, their beauty and their stuff of reality will always remain inseparable from the tangible and verifiable

truth of the Gospel event. The mystical Christ, the universal
Christ of St. Paul, has neither meaning nor value in our eyes
except as an expansion of the Christ who was born of Mary
and who died on the Cross. The former essentially draws His
fundamental quality of undeniability and concreteness from
the latter. However far we may be drawn into the divine spaces
opened up to us by Christian mysticism, we never depart from
the Jesus of the Gospels. On the contrary, we feel a growing
need to enfold ourselves ever more firmly within His human
truth. We are not, therefore, modernist in the condemned sense
of the word. Nor shall we end up among the visionaries and the
'illuminati.'

The real error of the visionaries is to *confuse* the different
planes of the world, and consequently to mix up their activities. In the view of the visionary, the divine presence illumi-
nates not only the heart of things, but tends to invade their
surface and hence to do away with their exacting but salutary
reality. The gradual maturing of immediate causes, the complex network of material determinisms, the infinite susceptibil-
ities of the universal order, no longer count. Through this veil
without seam and these delicate threads, divine action is imagined as appearing naked and without order. And then the falsely
miraculous comes to disconcert and obstruct the human effort.

As we have already abundantly shown, the effect produced
upon human activity, by the true transformation of the world
in Jesus Christ, is utterly different. At the heart of the divine
milieu, as the Church reveals it, things are transfigured, but
from within. They bathe inwardly in light, but, in this incandescence, they retain—this is not strong enough, they exalt
—all that is most specific in their attributes. *We can only lose
ourselves in God by prolonging the most individual characteristics of beings far beyond themselves:* that is the fundamental
rule by which we can always distinguish the true mystic from

his counterfeits. The heart of God is boundless, *multae man-siones*. And yet in all that immensity there is only one possible place for each one of us at any given moment, the one we are led to by unflagging fidelity to the natural and supernatural duties of life. At this point, which we can reach at the right moment only if we exert the maximum effort on every plane, God will reveal Himself in all His plenitude. Except at this point, the divine milieu, although it may still enfold us, exists only incompletely, or not at all, *for us*. Thus its great waters do not call us to defeat but to perpetual struggle to breast their floods. Their energy awaits, and provokes, our energy. Just as on certain days the sea lights up only as the ship's prow or the swimmer cleaves its surface, so the world is lit up with God only when reacting to our impetus. When God desires ultimately to subject and unite the Christian to Him, either by ecstasy or by death, it is as though He bears him away stiffened by love and by obedience in the full extent of his effort.

It might thenceforward look as though the believer in the divine milieu were falling back into the errors of a pagan naturalism in reaction against the excesses of quietism and illuminism. With his faith in the heavenly value of human endeavour, by his expectation of a new awakening of the faculties of adoration dormant in the world, by his respect for the spiritual powers still latent in matter, the Christian may often bear a striking resemblance to the worshippers of the earth.

But here again, as in the case of pantheism, the resemblance is only external and *such as is so often found in opposite things*.

The pagan loves the earth in order to enjoy it and confine himself within it; the Christian in order to make it purer and draw from it the strength to escape from it.

The pagan seeks to espouse sensible things so as to extract delight from them; *he adheres to the world*. The Christian multiplies his contacts with the world only so as to harness, or submit to, the energies which he will take back, or which will take him, to Heaven. *He pre-adheres to God.*

The pagan holds that man divinises himself by closing in upon himself; the final act of human evolution comes when the individual, or the totality, constitutes itself within itself. The Christian sees his divinisation only in the assimilation by an 'Other' of his achievement: the culmination of life, in his eyes, is death in union.

To the pagan, universal reality exists only in so far as it is projected on to the plane of the tangible: it is immediate and multiple. The Christian makes use of exactly the same elements: but he prolongs them along their common axis, which links them to God: and, by the same token, the universe is thus unified for him, although it is only attainable at the final centre of its consummation.

To sum up, one may say that, in relation to all the main historical forms assumed by the human religious spirit, Christian mysticism extracts *all* that is sweetest and strongest circulating in all the human mysticisms, though without absorbing their evil or suspect elements. It shows an astonishing equilibrium between the active and the passive, between possession of the world and its renunciation, between a taste for things and an indifference to them. But there is really no reason why we should be astonished by this shifting harmony, for is it not the natural and spontaneous reaction of the soul to the stimulus of a milieu which is exactly, by nature and grace, the one in which that soul is made to live and develop itself? Just as, at the centre of the divine milieu, all the sounds of created being are fused, without being confused, in a single note which dominates and sustains them (that seraphic note, no doubt, which bewitched St. Francis), so all the powers of the soul begin to resound in response to its call; and these multiple tones, in their turn, compose themselves into a single, ineffably simple vibration in which all the spiritual nuances— of love and of the intellect, of zeal and of tranquillity, of fullness and of ecstasy, of passion and of indifference, of assimilation and of surrender, of rest and of motion—are born and pass and shine forth, according to the times and the circumstances, like the countless possibilities of an inward attitude, inexpressible and unique.

And if any words could translate that permanent and lucid intoxication better than others, perhaps they would be 'passionate indifference.'

To have access to the divine milieu is to have found the One Thing needful: *Him who burns* by setting fire to everything that we would love badly or not enough; *Him who calms* by eclipsing with His blaze everything that we would love too much; *Him who consoles* by gathering up everything that has been snatched from our love or has never been given to it. To reach those priceless layers is to experience, with equal truth, that one has need of everything, and that one has need of nothing. Everything is needed because the world will never be large enough to provide our taste for action with the means of grasping God, or our thirst for undergoing with the possibility of being invaded by Him. And yet nothing is needed; for as the only reality which can satisfy us lies beyond the transparencies in which it is mirrored, everything that fades away and dies between us and it will only serve to give reality back to us with greater purity. Everything means both everything and nothing to me; everything is God to me and everything is dust to me: that is what man can say with equal truth, in accord with how the divine ray falls.

'Which is the greater blessing,' someone once asked, 'to have the sublime unity of God to centre and save the universe?

or to have the concrete immensity of the universe by which
to undergo and touch God?'

We shall not seek to escape this joyful uncertainty. But now
that we are familiar with the attributes of the divine milieu,
we shall turn our attention to the thing itself which appeared
to us in the depth of each being, like a radiant countenance,
like a fascinating abyss. We can now say 'Lord, who art Thou?'

2. The Nature of the Divine Milieu. The Universal Christ and the Great Communion

We can say as a first approximation that the milieu whose
rich and mobile homogeneity has revealed itself all around us
as a condition and a consequence of the most Christian attitudes (such as right intention and resignation) is formed by
the divine omnipresence. The immensity of God is the essential
attribute which allows us to seize Him everywhere, within us
and around us.

This answer begins to satisfy our minds in that it circum-
scribes the problem. However, it does not give to the power
in qua vivimus et sumus the sharp lines with which we should
wish to trace the features of the one thing needful. Under what
form, proper to our creation and adapted to our universe, does
the divine immensity manifest itself to, and become relevant
to, mankind? We feel it charged with that sanctifying grace
which the Catholic faith causes to circulate everywhere as the
true sap of the world; which, in its attributes, is very like that
charity (*Manete in dilectione mea*) which will one day, the
Scriptures tell us, be the only stable principle of natures and
powers; which, too, is fundamentally similar to the wonderful

and substantial divine will, whose marrow is everywhere present
and constitutes the true food of our lives, *omne delectamentum
in se habentem*. What is, when all is said and done, the concrete
link which binds all these universal entities together and confers on them a final power of gaining hold of us?

The essence of Christianity consists in asking oneself that
question, and in answering: 'The Word Incarnate, Our Lord
Jesus Christ.'

Let us examine step by step how we can justify to ourselves
this prodigious identification of the Son of Man and the divine
milieu.

A first step, unquestionably, is to see the divine omnipresence
in which we find ourselves plunged as *an omnipresence of action*. God enfolds us and penetrates us by creating and pre-
serving us.

Now let us go a little further. Under what form, and with
what end in view, has the Creator given us, and still preserves
in us, the gift of participated being? Under the form of an
essential aspiration towards Him—and with a view to the un-
hoped-for cleaving which is to make us one and the same
complex thing with Him. The action by which God maintains
us in the field of His presence is *a unitive transformation*.

Let us go further still. What is the supreme and complex
reality for which the divine operation moulds us? It is revealed
to us by St. Paul and St. John. It is the quantitative repletion
and the qualitative consummation of all things: it is the mysterious Pleroma, in which the substantial *One* and the created
many fuse without confusion in a *whole* which, without adding
anything essential to God, will nevertheless be a sort of triumph
and generalisation of being.

At last we are nearing our goal. What is the active centre,
the living link, the organising soul of the Pleroma? St. Paul,
again, proclaims it with all his resounding voice: it is He in

whom everything is reunited, and in whom all things are consummated—through whom the whole created edifice receives
its consistency—Christ dead and risen *qui replet omnia, in quo
omnia constant.*

And now let us link the first and last terms of this long
series of identities. We shall then see with a wave of joy
that *the divine omnipresence* translates itself within our universe by the network of the organising forces of the total Christ.
God exerts pressure, in us and upon us—through the intermedi-
ary of all the powers of heaven, earth and hell—only in the
act of forming and consummating Christ who saves and sur-
animates the world. And since, in the course of this operation,
Christ Himself does not act as a dead or passive point of convergence, but as a centre of radiation for the energies which
lead the universe back to God through His humanity, the layers
of divine action finally come to us impregnated with His organic
energies.

The divine milieu henceforward assumes for us the savour
and the specific features which we desire. In it we recognise
an omnipresence which acts upon us by assimilating us in it,
in unitate corporis Christi. As a consequence of the Incarnation,
the divine immensity has transformed itself for us into *the
omnipresence of christification.* All the good that I can do *opus
et operatio* is physically gathered in, by something of itself,
into the reality of the consummated Christ. Everything I endure, with faith and love, by way of diminishment or death,
makes me a little more closely an integral part of His mystical
body. Quite specifically it is *Christ whom we make or whom
we undergo in all things.* Not only *diligentibus omnia convertuntur in bonum* but, more clearly still, *convertuntur in
Deum* and, quite explicitly, *convertuntur in Christum.*

In spite of the strength of St. Paul's expressions (formulated,
it should be remembered, for the *ordinary run* of the first Chris-

tians) some readers may feel that we have been led to strain, in too realist a direction, the meaning of 'Mystical Body'—or at least that we have allowed ourselves to seek esoteric perspectives in it. But if we look a little more closely, we shall see that we have simply taken another path in order to rejoin the great highway opened up in the Church by the onrush of the cult of the Holy Eucharist.

When the priest says the words *Hoc est Corpus meum*, his words fall directly on to the bread and directly transform it into the individual reality of Christ. But the great sacramental operation does not cease at that local and momentary event. Even children are taught that, throughout the life of each man and the life of the Church and the history of the world, there is only one Mass and one Communion. Christ died once in agony. Peter and Paul receive communion on such and such a day at a particular hour. But these different acts are only the diversely central points in which the continuity of a unique act is split up and fixed, in space and time, for our experience. In fact, from the beginning of the Messianic preparation, up till the Parousia, passing through the historic manifestation of Jesus and the phases of growth of His Church, a single event has been developing in the world: the Incarnation, realised, in each individual, through the Eucharist.

All the communions of a life-time are one communion.

All the communions of all men now living are one communion.

All the communions of all men, present, past and future, are one communion.

Have we ever sufficiently considered the physical immensity of man, and his extraordinary relations with the universe, in order to realise in our minds the formidable implications of this elementary truth?

Let us conjure up in our minds, as best we can, the vast

multitudes of men in every epoch and in every land. According to the catechism we believe that this fearful anonymous throng is, by right, subject to the physical and overmastering contact of Him whose appanage it is to be able *omnia sibi subicere* (by right, and to a certain extent in fact; for who can tell where the diffusion of Christ, with the influence of grace, stops, as it spreads outward from the faithful at the heart of the human family?). Yes, the human layer of the earth is wholly and continuously under the organising influx of the Incarnate Christ. This we all believe, as one of the most certain points of our faith.

Now how does the human world itself appear within the structure of the universe? We have already spoken of this (pp. 27 ff), and the more one thinks of it the more one is struck by the obviousness and importance of the following conclusions: it appears as a zone of continuous spiritual transformation, where all inferior realities and forces without exception are sublimated into sensations, feelings, ideas and the powers of knowledge and love. Around the earth, the centre of our field of vision, the souls of men form, in some manner, the incandescent surface of matter plunged in God. From the dynamic and biological point of view it is quite as impossible to draw a line below it, as to draw a line between a plant and the environment that sustains it. If, then, the Eucharist is a sovereign influence upon our human natures, then its energy necessarily extends, owing to the effects of continuity, into the less luminous regions that sustain us; *descendit ad inferos*, one might say. At every moment the Eucharistic Christ controls— from the point of view of the organisation of the Pleroma (which is the only true point of view from which the world can be understood)—the whole movement of the universe: the Christ *per quem omnia, Domine, semper creas, vivificas et praestas nobis*.

The control of which we are speaking is, at the minimum,
a final refinement, a final purification, a final harnessing, of all
the elements which can be used in the construction of the New
Earth. But how can we avoid going further and believing that
the sacramental action of Christ, *precisely because it sanctifies
matter*, extends its influence beyond the pure supernatural, over
all that makes up the internal and external ambiance of the
faithful, that is to say that it sets its mark in everything which
we call 'our Providence'?

If this is the case, then we find ourselves (by simply having
followed the 'extensions' of the Eucharist) plunged once again
precisely into our divine milieu. Christ—for whom and in whom
we are formed, each with his own individuality and his own
vocation—Christ reveals Himself in each reality around us, and
shines like an ultimate determinant, like a centre, one might
almost say like a universal element. As our humanity assimilates the material world, and as the Host assimilates our humanity, the eucharistic transformation goes beyond and com-
pletes the transubstantiation of the bread on the altar. Step
by step it irresistibly invades the universe. It is the fire that
sweeps over the heath; the stroke that vibrates through the
bronze. In a secondary and generalised sense, but in a true
sense, the sacramental Species are formed by the totality of
the world, and the duration of the creation is the time needed
for its consecration. *In Christo vivimus, movemur et sumus.*

*Grant, O God, that when I draw near to the altar to com-
municate, I may henceforth discern the infinite perspectives
hidden beneath the smallness and the nearness of the Host in
which You are concealed. I have already accustomed myself
to seeing, beneath the stillness of that piece of bread, a devour-
ing power which, in the words of the greatest Doctors of Your*

*Church, far from being consumed by me, consumes me. Give
me the strength to rise above the remaining illusions which tend
to make me think of Your touch as circumscribed and momentary.*

*I am beginning to understand: under the sacramental Species
it is primarily through the 'accidents' of matter that You touch
me, but, as a consequence, it is also through the whole universe
in proportion as this ebbs and flows over me under Your primary
influence. In a true sense the arms and the heart which You
open to me are nothing less than all the united powers of the
world which, penetrated and permeated to their depths by Your
will, Your tastes and Your temperament, converge upon my
being to form it, nourish it and bear it along towards the centre
of Your fire. In the Host it is my life that You are offering me,
O Jesus.*

*What can I do to gather up and answer that universal and
enveloping embrace? Quomodo comprehendam ut comprehen-
sus sum? To the total offer that is made me, I can only answer
by a total acceptance. I shall therefore react to the eucharistic
contact with the entire effort of my life—of my life of today
and of my life of tomorrow, of my personal life and of my life
as linked to all other lives. Periodically, the sacred Species may
perhaps fade away in me. But each time they will leave me a
little more deeply engulfed in the layers of Your omnipresence:
living and dying, I shall never at any moment cease to move
forward in You. Thus the precept implicit in Your Church,
that we must communicate everywhere and always, is justified
with extraordinary force and precision. The Eucharist must invade my life. My life must become, as a result of the sacrament,
an unlimited and endless contact with You—that life which
seemed, a few moments ago, like a Baptism with You in the
waters of the world, now reveals itself to me as communion with*

You through the world. It is the sacrament of life. The sacrament of my life— *of my life received, of my life lived, of my life surrendered* . . .

Because You ascended into heaven after having descended into hell, You have so filled the universe in every direction, Jesus, that henceforth it is blessedly impossible for us to escape You. Quo ibo a spiritu tuo, et quo a facie tua fugiam. *Now I know that for certain. Neither life, whose advance increases Your hold upon me; nor death, which throws me into Your hands; nor the good or evil spiritual powers which are Your living instruments; nor the energies of matter into which You have plunged; nor the irreversible stream of duration, whose rhythm and flow You control without appeal; nor the unfathomable abysses of space which are the measure of Your greatness,* neque mors, neque vita, neque angeli, neque principatus, neque potestates, neque virtutes, neque instantia, neque futura, neque fortitudo, neque altitudo, neque profundum, neque ulla creatura [1]—*none of these things will be able to separate me from Your substantial love, because they are all only the veil, the 'species,' under which You take hold of me in order that I may take hold of You.*

Once again, Lord, I ask which is the most precious of these two beatitudes: that all things for me should be a contact with You? or that You should be so 'universal' that I can undergo You and grasp You in every creature?

Sometimes people think that they can increase Your attraction in my eyes by stressing almost exclusively the charm and goodness of Your human life in the past. But truly, O Lord, if I wanted to cherish only a man, then I would surely turn to those whom You have given me in the allurement of their present flowering. Are there not, with our mothers, brothers, friends

---

[1] Rom. viii, 38.

and sisters, enough irresistibly lovable people around us? Why should we turn to Judaea two thousand years ago? No, what I cry out for, like every being, with my whole life and all my earthly passion, is something very different from an equal to cherish: it is a God to adore.

To adore . . . That means to lose oneself in the unfathomable, to plunge into the inexhaustible, to find peace in the incorruptible, to be absorbed in defined immensity, to offer oneself to the fire and the transparency, to annihilate oneself in proportion as one becomes more deliberately conscious of oneself, and to give of one's deepest to that whose depth has no end. Whom, then, can we adore?

The more man becomes man, the more will he become prey to a need, a need that is always more explicit, more subtle and more magnificent, the need to adore.

Disperse, O Jesus, the clouds with Your lightning! Show Yourself to us as the Mighty, the Radiant, the Risen! Come to us once again as the Pantocrator who filled the solitude of the cupolas in the ancient basilicas! Nothing less than this Parousia is needed to counter-balance and dominate in our hearts the glory of the world that is coming into view. And so that we should triumph over the world with You, come to us clothed in the glory of the world.

3. The Growth of the Divine Milieu

The Kingdom of God is within us. When Christ appears in the clouds He will simply be manifesting a metamorphosis that has been slowly accomplished under His influence in the heart of the mass of mankind. In order to hasten His coming, let us therefore concentrate upon a better understanding of the process by which the Holy Presence is born and grows within us. In order to foster its progress more intelligently let us observe the birth and growth of the divine milieu, first in ourselves and then in the world that begins with us.

A. *The coming of the divine milieu. The taste for being and the diaphany of God*

A breeze passes in the night. When did it spring up? Whence does it come? Whither is it going? No man knows. No one can compel the spirit, the gaze or the light of God to descend upon him.

On some given day a man suddenly becomes conscious that he is alive to a particular perception of the divine spread everywhere about him. Question him. When did this state begin for him? He cannot tell. All he knows is that a new spirit has crossed his life.

'It began with a particular and unique resonance which swelled each harmony, with a diffused radiance which haloed each beauty . . . All the elements of psychological life were in turn affected; sensations, feelings, thoughts. Day by day they became more fragrant, more coloured, more intense by means of an indefinable thing—the same thing. Then the vague note, and fragrance, and light began to define themselves. And then, contrary to all expectation and all probability, I began to feel what was ineffably common to all things. The unity communicated itself to me by giving me the gift of grasping it. I had in fact acquired a new sense, *the sense of a new quality* or *of a new dimension.* Deeper still: a transformation had taken place for me *in the very perception of being.* Thenceforward being had become, in some way, tangible and savorous to me; and as it came to dominate all the forms which it assumed, being itself began to draw me and to intoxicate me.'

That is what any man might say, more or less explicitly, who has gone any distance in the development of his capacity for self-analysis. Outwardly he could well be a pagan. And should he happen to be a Christian, he would admit that this inward reversal seemed to him to have occurred within the profane and 'natural' parts of his soul.

But we must not allow ourselves to be deceived by appearances. We must not let ourselves be disconcerted by the patent errors into which many mystics have fallen in their attempts to place and even to name the universal Smile. As with all power (and the richer, the more so) the sense of the All comes to birth inchoate and troubled. It often happens that, like children opening their eyes for the first time, men do not accurately place the reality which they sense behind things. Their gropings often meet with nothing but a metaphysical phantom or a crude idol. But images and reflections have never proved anything against the reality of objects and of the light. The false trails of pantheism bear witness to our immense need for some revealing word to come from the mouth of Him who is. With that reservation, it remains true that, physiologically, the so-called 'natural' taste for being is, in each life, the first dawn of the divine illumination—the first tremor perceived of the world animated by the Incarnation. The sense (*which is not necessarily the feeling*) of the omnipresence of God prolongs, sur-creates and supernaturalises the identical physiological energy which, in a mutilated or misdirected form, produces the various styles of pantheism.[1]

---

[1] In other words and more simply: Just as in the love of God (Charity) can be found, quite obviously, the human power to love in its supernatural state—so, in the same way, we believe that at the psychological origin of the 'feeling of omnipresence,' experienced by the Christian can be found 'the sense of universal Being' which is the source of the majority of human mysticisms. There is a soul which is *naturaliter christiana*. It should be remembered (cf. the Introduction) that these pages contain a psychological description, not a theological explanation, of the states of soul met with.

Once we realise that the *divine milieu discloses itself to us as a modification of the deep being of things*, it is at once possible to make two important observations touching the manner in which its perception is introduced and preserved within our human horizons.

In the first place, the manifestation of the divine no more modifies the apparent order of things than the eucharistic consecration modifies the sacred Species to our eyes. Since the psychological event consists, at first, solely in the appearance of an *inward tension* or *deep brilliance*, the relations between creatures remains exactly the same. They are merely accentuated in meaning. Like those translucent materials which a light within them can illuminate as a whole, the world appears to the Christian mystic bathed in an inward light which intensifies its relief, its structure and its depth. This light is not the superficial glimmer which can be realised in coarse enjoyment. Nor is it the violent flash which destroys objects and blinds our eyes. It is the calm and powerful radiance engendered by the synthesis of all the elements of the world in Jesus. The more fulfilled, according to their nature, are the beings in whom it comes to play, the closer and more sensible this radiance appears; and the more sensible it becomes, the more the objects which it bathes become distinct in contour and remote in substance. If we may slightly alter a hallowed expression, we could say that the great mystery of Christianity is not exactly the appearance, but the transparence, of God in the universe. Yes, Lord, not only the ray that strikes the surface, but the ray that penetrates, not only Your Epiphany, Jesus, but *Your diaphany*.

Nothing is more consistent or more fleeting—more fused with things or at the same time more separable from them—than a ray of light. If the divine milieu reveals itself to us as an incandescence of the inward layers of being, who is to guarantee us the persistence of this vision? No one other than the Ray of light itself. The diaphany . . . No power in the world can prevent us from savouring its joys because it happens at a level deeper than any power; and no power in the world—for the same reason—can compel it to appear.

That is the second point, the consideration of which should be used as the basis for all our further reflections on the progress of life in God.

The perception of the divine omnipresence is essentially a seeing, a taste, that is to say a sort of intuition bearing upon certain superior qualities in things. It cannot, therefore, be attained directly by any process of reasoning, nor by any human artifice. It is a gift, like life itself, of which it is undoubtedly the supreme experimental perfection. And so we are brought back again to the centre of ourselves, to the edge of that mysterious source to which we descended (at the beginning of Part Two and watched it as it welled up. To experience the attraction of God, to be sensible of the beauty, the consistency and the final unity of being, is the highest and at the same time the most complete of our 'passivities of growth.' God tends, by the logic of His creative effort, to make Himself sought and perceived by us: *Posuit homines . . . si forte attrectent eum.* His prevenient grace is therefore always on the alert to excite our first look and our first prayer. But in the end the initiative, the awakening, always come from Him, and whatever the further developments of our mystical faculties, no progress is achieved in this domain except as the new response to a new gift. *Nemo venit ad me, nisi Pater traxerit eum.*

We are thus led to posit intense and continual prayer at the origin of our invasion by the divine milieu, the prayer which begs for the fundamental gift: *Domine, fac ut videam.* Lord, we know and feel that You are everywhere around us; but it seems that there is a veil before our eyes. *Illumina vultum tuum super nos*—let the light of Your countenance shine upon us in its

universality. *Sit splendor Domini nostri super nos*—may Your
deep brilliance light up the innermost parts of the massive
obscurities in which we move. And, to that end, send us Your
spirit, *Spiritus principalis*, whose flaming action alone can operate the birth and achievement of the great metamorphosis
which sums up all inward perfection and towards which Your
creation yearns: *Emitte Spiritum tuum, et creabuntur, et
RENOVABIS FACIEM TERRAE.*

B. Individual progress in the divine milieu: purity, faith and fidelity, the operatives

Ego operor . . . Pater semper operatur. The charm of the
divine milieu (heavy with responsibilities) is that it can assume
an *ever increasing* intensity around us. One could say that it
is an atmosphere ever more luminous and ever more charged
with God. It is in Him and in Him alone that the reckless vow
of all love is realised: to lose oneself in what one loves, to
sink oneself in it more and more.

It could be said that three virtues contribute with particular
effectiveness towards the limitless concentration of the divine
in our lives—purity, faith and fidelity; three virtues which appear
to be 'static' but which are in fact the three most active and
unconfined virtues of all. Let us look at them one after the
other, and examine their generative function in the divine
milieu.

i. Purity

Purity, in the wide sense of the word, is not merely the ab-
staining from wrong (that is only a negative aspect of purity),
nor even chastity (which is only a remarkable special instance of
it). It is the rectitude and the impulse introduced into our lives
by the love of God sought in and above everything.

He is spiritually impure who, lingering in pleasure or shut up in selfishness, introduces, within himself and around himself, a principle of slowing-down and division in the unification of the universe in God.

He is pure, on the other hand, who, in accord with his place in the world, seeks to give Christ's desire to consummate all things precedence over his own immediate and momentary advantage.

Still purer and more pure is he who, attracted by God, succeeds in giving that movement and impulse of Christ's an ever greater continuity, intensity and reality—whether his vocation calls him to move always in the material zones of the world (though more and more spiritually), or whether, as is more often the case, he has access to regions where the divine gradually replaces for him all other earthly nourishment.

Thus understood, the purity of beings is measured by the degree of the attraction that draws them towards the divine centre, or, what comes to the same thing, by their proximity to the centre. Christian experience teaches us that it is preserved by recollection, mental prayer, purity of conscience, purity of intention and the sacraments. Let us be satisfied, here, with extolling its wonderful power of condensing the divine in all around us.

In one of his stories, Robert Hugh Benson tells of a 'visionary' coming on a lonely chapel where a nun is praying. He enters. All at once he sees the whole world bound up and moving and organising itself around that out-of-the-way spot, in tune with the intensity and inflection of the desires of that puny praying figure. The convent chapel had become the axis about which the earth revolved. The contemplative sensitised and animated all things because she believed; and her faith was operative because her very pure soul placed her near to God. This piece of fiction is an admirable parable.

The inward tension of the mind towards God may seem negligible to those who try to calculate the quantity of energy accumulated in the mass of humanity.

And yet, if we could see the 'light invisible' as we can see clouds or lightning or the rays of the sun, a pure soul would seem as active in this world, by virtue of its sheer purity, as the snowy summits whose impassible peaks breathe in continually for us the roving powers of the high atmosphere.

If we want the divine milieu to grow all around us, then we must jealously guard and nourish all the forces of union, of desire, and of prayer that grace offers us. By the mere fact that our transparency will increase, the divine light, that never ceases to press in upon us, will irrupt the more powerfully.

Have we ever thought of the meaning of the mystery of the Annunciation?

When the time had come when God resolved to realise His Incarnation before our eyes, He had first of all to raise up in the world a virtue capable of drawing Him as far as ourselves. He needed a mother who would engender Him in the human sphere. What did He do? He created the Virgin Mary, that is to say He called forth on earth a purity so great that, within this transparency, He would concentrate Himself to the point of appearing as a child.

There, expressed in its strength and reality, is the power of purity to bring the divine to birth among us.

And yet the Church, addressing the Virgin Mother, adds: *Beata quae credidisti*. For it is in faith that purity finds the fulfilment of its fertility.

ii. Faith

Faith, as we understand it here, is not—of course—simply the intellectual adherence to Christian dogma. It is taken in a much richer sense to mean belief in God charged with all the trust in His beneficent strength that the knowledge of the divine Being arouses in us. It means the practical conviction that the universe, between the hands of the Creator, still continues to be the clay in which He shapes innumerable possibilities according to His will. In a word, it is *evangelical faith,* of which it can be said that no virtue, not even charity, was more strongly urged by the Saviour.

Now, under what guise was this disposition so untiringly revealed to us by the words and deeds of the Master? Above all and beyond all, as *an operative power.* But, intimidated by the assertions of an unproven positivism, or 'put off' by the mystical excesses of Christian Science, we are sometimes tempted to gloss over the disconcerting promise that the efficacy of prayer is tangible and certain. Yet we cannot ignore it without blushing for Christ. If we do not believe, the waves engulf us, the winds blow, nourishment fails, sickness lays us low or kills us, the divine power is impotent or remote. If, on the other hand, we believe, the waters are welcoming and sweet, the bread is multiplied, our eyes open, the dead rise again, the power of God is, as it were, drawn from Him by force and spreads throughout all nature. One must either arbitrarily minimise or explain away the Gospel, or one must admit the reality of these effects not as transient and past, but as perennial and actually true. Let us beware of stifling this revelation of a possible vitalisation of the forces of nature in God. Let us, rather, place it resolutely at the centre of our vision of the world—careful, only, that we understand it aright.

When we say that faith is 'operative,' what do we mean? Is divine action, at the call of faith, going to replace the normal interplay of the causes which surround us? Do we, like the 'illuminati,' expect God to bring about directly, upon matter or upon our bodies, results that have hitherto been obtained by our own industrious research?

Obviously not. Neither the internal inter-relations of the material or psychical world, nor man's duty to make the greatest possible effort, are in any way undermined, or even relaxed, by the precepts of faith. *Iota unum aut unus apex non praeteribit.* All the natural links of the world remain intact under the transforming action of 'operative faith'; but a principle, an inward finality, one might almost say an additional soul, is superimposed upon them. Under the influence of our faith, the universe is capable, without outwardly changing its characteristics, of becoming more supple, more fully animate—of being 'sur-animated.' That is the 'at the most' and the 'at the least' of the belief expressly imposed upon us by the Gospel. Sometimes this 'sur-animation' expresses itself in miraculous effects—when the transfiguration of causes permits them access to the zone of their 'obediential potency.' At other times, and this is the more usual case, it is manifested by the integration of unimportant or unfavorable events within a higher plane and within a higher providence.

We have already mentioned and analysed (p. 58) a very typical example of this second form of divinisation of the world by faith (a form no less profound and no less precious than more striking prodigies). In considering the passivities of diminishment we saw how our failures, our death, our faults even, could—through God—be recast into something better and transformed in Him. The moment has come to envisage this miracle in its most general sense and from the particular point of view of the act of faith which is, on our part, its providential condition.

In our hands, in the hands of all of us, the world and life (*our world, our life*) are placed like a Host, ready to be charged with the divine influence, that is to say with a real Presence of the Incarnate Word. The mystery will be accomplished. But on one condition: which is that *we shall believe* that *this* has the

will and the power to become for us the action—that is to say
the prolongation of the Body of Christ. If we believe, then
everything is illuminated and takes shape around us: chance is
seen to be order, success assumes an incorruptible plenitude,
suffering becomes a visit and a caress of God. But if we hesitate, the rock remains dry, the sky dark, the waters treacherous
and shifting. And we may hear the voice of the Master, faced
with our bungled lives: 'O men of little faith, why have you
doubted . . . ?'

Domine, adjuva incredulitatem meam. *Ah, You know it
Yourself, Lord, through having borne the anguish of it as man:
on certain days the world seems a terrifying thing: huge, blind
and brutal. It buffets us about, drags us along, and kills us with
complete indifference.* Heroically, it may truly be said, man has
contrived to create a more or less habitable zone of light and
warmth in the midst of the great, cold, black waters—a zone
where people have eyes to see, hands to help, and hearts to love.
But how precarious that habitation is! At any moment the vast
and horrible thing may break in through the cracks—the thing
which we try hard to forget is always there, separated from us
by a flimsy partition: fire, pestilence, storms, earthquakes, or
the unleashing of dark moral forces—these callously sweep away
in one moment what we had laboriously built up and beautified
with all our intelligence and all our heart.

*Since human dignity, O God, forbids me to close my eyes to
this—like a beast or a child—that I may not succumb to the
temptation to curse the universe and Him who made it,* teach
me to adore it by seeing You concealed within it. *O Lord, repeat
to me the great liberating words, the words which at once reveal
and operate:* Hoc est Corpus meum. *In truth, the huge and dark
Thing, the phantom, the storm—if we want it to be so, is You!*
Ego sum, nolite timere. *The things in our life which terrify us,*

*the things that threw You Yourself into agony in the Garden,
are, ultimately, only the Species or Appearance, the matter of
one and the same Sacrament.*

We have only to believe. And the more threatening and irre-
ducible reality appears, the more firmly and desperately must
we believe. Then, little by little, we shall see the universal horror
unbend, and then smile upon us, and then take us in its more
than human arms.

No, it is not the rigid determinism of matter and of large
numbers, but the subtle combinations of the Spirit, that give
the universe its consistency. The immense hazard and the immense blindness of the world are only an illusion to him who
believes. *Fides, substantia rerum.*

iii. Fidelity

Because we have believed intensely and with a pure heart in
the world, the world will open the arms of God to us. It is
for us to throw ourselves into these arms so that the divine
milieu should close around our lives like a circle. That gesture
of ours will be one of an active response to our daily tasks. *Faith
consecrates the world. Fidelity communicates with it.*

To give a worthy description of the 'advantages' of fidelity,
that is to say of the essential and final part which it plays in
our taking possession of the divine milieu, we should have to
go back to what was said in the first two parts of this study.
For it is fidelity which releases the inexhaustible resources offered by every passion to our desire for communion.

Through fidelity we situate ourselves and maintain ourselves
in the hands of God so exactly as to become one with them
in their action.

Through fidelity we open ourselves so intimately and continuously to the wishes and good pleasure of God, that His life

penetrates and assimilates ours like a fortifying bread. *Hoc est cibus meus, ut faciam voluntatem Patris.*

And finally, through fidelity we find ourselves at every moment situated at the exact point at which the whole bundle of inward and outward forces of the world converge providentially upon us, that is to say at the one point where the divine milieu can, at a given moment, be made real for us.

It is fidelity and fidelity alone that enables us to welcome the universal and perpetual overtures of the divine milieu; through fidelity and fidelity alone can we return to God the kiss He is for ever offering us across the world.

What is without price in the 'communicating' power of fidelity is that, like the power possessed by faith and purity, it knows no limit to its efficacy.

There is no limit *in respect of the work* done or the diminishment undergone, because we can always sink ourselves deeper into the perfecting of work to be achieved, or into the better utilisation of distressing events. We can always be more industrious, more meticulous, more flexible . . .

Nor is there any limit *in respect of the intention* which animates our endeavour to act or to accept, because we can always go further in the inward perfecting of our conformity. There can always be greater detachment and greater love.

And there is no limit, indeed there is still less limit, *in respect of the divine object* in the ever closer espousal of which our being can joyfully wear itself away. This is the moment to abandon all conception of static adherence; it can only be inadequate. And let us remember this: God does not offer Himself to our finite beings as a thing all complete and ready to be embraced. For us He is eternal discovery and eternal growth. The more we think we understand Him, the more He reveals Himself as otherwise. The more we think we hold Him, the further He withdraws, drawing us into the depths of Himself.

The nearer we approach Him through all the efforts of nature and grace, the more He increases, in one and the same movement, His attraction over our powers, and the receptivity of our powers to that divine attraction.

Thus the privileged point which was mentioned a short time back—the one point at which the divine milieu may be born, for each man, at each moment—is not a fixed point in the universe, but a moving centre which we have to follow, like the Magi their star.

That star leads each man differently, by a different path, in accord with his vocation. But all the paths which it indicates have this in common: that they lead always upward. (We have already said these things more than once, but it is important to group them together for the last time in the same bundle.) In any existence, if it has fidelity, greater desires follow on lesser ones, renunciation gradually gains mastery over pleasure, death consummates life. Finally the general drift throughout creation will have been the same for all. Sometimes through detachment of mind, sometimes through effective detachment, fidelity leads us all, more or less fast and more or less far, towards the same zone of minimal egoism and minimal pleasure— to where, for the more ecstatic creature, the divine light glows with greater amplitude and greater limpidity, beyond the intermediaries which have been, *not rejected*, but *overcome*.

Under the converging action of these three rays—purity, faith and fidelity—the world melts and folds.

Like a huge fire that is fed by what should normally extinguish it, or like a mighty torrent which is swelled by the very obstacles placed to stem it, so the tension engendered by the encounter between man and God dissolves, bears along and volatilises created things and makes them all, equally, serve the cause of union.

Joys, advances, sufferings, setbacks, mistakes, works, prayers, beauties, the powers of heaven, earth and hell—everything bows down under the touch of the heavenly waves; and everything yields up the portion of positive energy contained within its nature so as to contribute to the richness of the divine milieu.

Like the jet of flame that effortlessly pierces the hardest metal, so the spirit drawn to God penetrates through the world and makes its way enveloped in the luminous vapours of what it sublimates with Him.

It does not destroy things, nor distort them; but it liberates things, directs them, transfigures them, animates them. It does not leave things behind but, as it rises, it leans on them for support; and carries along with it the chosen part in things.

Purity, faith and fidelity, static virtues and operative virtues, you are truly, in your serenity, nature's noblest energies—those which give even the material world its final consistency and its ultimate shape. You are the formative principles of the New Earth. Through you, three-fold aspect of a same trusting adoration, 'we shall overcome the world': Haec est quae vincit mundum, fides nostra.

C. *The collective progress of the divine milieu.* *The communion of saints and charity*

i. Preliminary remarks on the 'individual' value of the divine milieu

In the foregoing pages we have been concerned in practice with the establishment and progress of the divine milieu in a soul envisaged alone in the world in the presence of God. 'But what about its relationship to other people?' more than one reader must have thought; 'where do other people come in? What sort of Christianity is this, that thinks it can build up an edifice without regard to love of neighbour?'

Our neighbour, as will now be seen, has an essential place in the edifice whose general outline we have tried to trace. But, before we could insert him within its structure, we had to deal thoroughly with the problem of the 'divinisation of the world' in the particular case of an individual man, and this for two reasons.

In the first place for reasons of *method*; for, by sound scientific rules, the study of particular cases must precede an attempt at generalisation.

In the second place, for reasons of *nature*; for whatever extraordinary solidarity we have with each other in our development and in our consummation *in Christo Jesu*, each of us forms, none the less, a natural unity charged with its own responsibilities and its own incommunicable possibilities within that consummation. It is *we* who save ourselves or lose ourselves.

It was all the more important to stress this Christian doctrine of individual salvation precisely as the perspectives developed here became more unitary and more universalist. It must never be forgotten that, as in the experimental spheres of the world each man, though enveloped within the same universe as all other men, presents an independent centre of perspective and activity for that universe (so that there are as many partial universes as there are individuals), so in the realm of heavenly realities, however deeply impregnated we may be by the same creative and redemptive force, each one of us constitutes a particular centre of divinisation (so that there are as many partial divine milieux as there are Christian souls).

Men, as we know, according to the dimness or perfection of their senses and intelligence, react so differently in the same circumstances and in the presence of the same opportunities of perception and action, that if *per impossibile* we could migrate from one consciousness into another we should each time change our world. In the same way, God presents and gives

Himself to our souls under the same temporal and spatial 'species,' but with very different degrees of reality and fullness, according to the faith, fidelity and purity which His influence encounters. An achievement or a disaster which involves a whole group of men has as many different facets, finalities and 'souls' as there are individuals involved: blind, absurd, indifferent or material to those who do not love and do not believe, it will be luminous, providential, charged with significance and love to those who have achieved seeing and touching God everywhere. There are as many sur-animations by God of secondary causes as there are forms of human trust and human fidelity. Although essentially single in its influx, Providence is pluralised when in contact with us—just as a ray of sunlight takes on colour or loses itself in the depths of the body which it strikes. The universe has many different storeys and many different compartments: *in eadem domo, multae mansiones.*

That is why, in repeating over *our* lives the words the priest says over the bread and wine before the consecration, we should pray, each one of us, that the world may be transfigured for our use: *ut nobis Corpus et Sanguinis fiat D.N. Jesu Christi.*

That is the first step. Before considering others (and in order to do so) the believer must make sure of his own personal sanctification—not out of egoism, but with a firm and broad understanding that the task of each one of us is to divinise the whole world in an infinitesimal and incommunicable degree.

We have tried to show how this partial divinisation is possible. It only remains for us to integrate the elemental phenomenon and see how the total divine milieu is formed by the confluence of our individual divine milieux, and how, in order to complete them, it reacts in its turn upon the particular destinies which it clasps in its embrace. The time has come to generalise our conclusions by multiplying them to infinity by the action of charity.

ii. The intensification of the divine milieu
through charity

In order to measure and understand the power of divinisation contained in love for one's neighbour, we must re-examine some of the themes already considered, and especially those passages in which we discussed the total unity of the eucharistic consecration.

Across the immensity of time and the disconcerting multiplicity of individuals, one single operation is taking place: the annexation to Christ of His chosen; one single thing is being made: the Mystical Body of Christ, starting from all the sketchy spiritual powers scattered throughout the world. *Hoc est Corpus meum.* Nobody in the world can save us, or lose us, in our despite; that is true. But it is also true that our salvation is not pursued or achieved except in *solidarity* with the justification of the whole 'body of the elect.' In a real sense, only one man will be saved: Christ, the Head and living summary of humanity. Each one of the elect is called to see God face to face. But his act of vision will be vitally inseparable from the elevating and illuminating action of Christ. In heaven we ourselves shall contemplate God, but, as it were, through the eyes of Christ.

If this is so, then our individual mystical effort awaits an essential completion in its union with the mystical effort of all other men. The divine milieu which will ultimately be one in the Pleroma, must begin to become one during the earthly phase of our existence. So that although the Christian who hungers to live in God may have attained all possible purity of desire, faith in prayer, and fidelity in action, the divinisation of his universe is still open to vast possibilities. It would still remain for him to link his elemental work to that of all the labourers who surround him. The innumerable partial worlds which envelop the diverse human monads press in upon him from all around. His task is to rekindle his own ardour by contact with the ardour of all these foci, to make his own sap communicate with that circulating in the other cells, to receive or propagate movement and life for the common benefit, and to adapt himself to the common temperature and tension.

To what power is it reserved to burst asunder the envelope in which our individual microcosms tend jealously to isolate themselves and vegetate? To what force is it given to merge and exalt our partial rays into the principal radiance of Christ?

To charity, the beginning and the end of all spiritual relationships. Christian charity, which is preached so fervently by the Gospels, is nothing else than the more or less conscious cohesion of souls engendered by their communal convergence *in Christo Jesu.* It is impossible to love Christ without loving others (in proportion as these others are moving towards Christ). And it is impossible to love others (in a spirit of broad human communion) without moving nearer to Christ. Hence automatically, by a sort of living determinism, the individual divine milieux, in proportion as they establish themselves, tend to fuse one with another; and in this association they find a boundless increase of their ardour. This inevitable conjunction of forces has always been manifested, in the interior lives of the saints, by an overflowing love for everything which, in creatures, carries in itself a germ of eternal life. We have already examined 'the tension of communion' and its wonderful efficacy for directing man towards his human duty. It enables him to extract life even from powers which seem most heavily charged with death, and its ultimate effect is to precipitate the Christian into the love of souls.

The man with a passionate sense of the divine milieu cannot bear to find things about him obscure, tepid and empty which should be full and vibrant with God. He is paralysed by the thought of the numberless spirits which are linked to his in the unity of the same world, but are not yet fully kindled by the flame of the divine Presence. He had thought for a time that he had only to stretch out his own hand in order to touch God to the measure of his desires. He now sees that the only human embrace capable of worthily enfolding the divine is that of all men opening their arms to call down and welcome the fire. The only subject ultimately capable of mystical transfiguration is the whole group of mankind forming a single body and a single soul in charity.

And this coalescence of the spiritual units of creation under the attraction of Christ is the supreme victory of faith over the world.

I confess, my God, that I have long been, and even now am, recalcitrant to the love of my neighbour. Just as much as I have derived intense joy in the superhuman delight of dissolving myself and losing myself in the souls for which I was destined by the mysterious affinities of human love, so I have always felt an inborn hostility to, and closed myself to, the common run of those whom You tell me to love. I find no difficulty in integrating into my inward life everything above and beneath me (in the same line as me, as it were) in the universe—whether matter, plants, animals, and then powers, dominions and angels: these I can accept without difficulty and delight to feel myself sustained within their hierarchy. But 'the other man,' my God— by which I do not mean 'the poor, the halt, the lame and the sick,' but 'the other' quite simply as 'other,' the one who seems to exist independently of me because his universe seems closed to mine, and who seems to shatter the unity and the silence of the world for me—would I be sincere if I did not confess that my instinctive reaction is to rebuff him? and that the mere thought of entering into spiritual communication with him disgusts me?

Grant, O God, that the light of Your countenance may shine for me in the life of that 'other.' The irresistible light of Your eyes shining in the depth of things has already guided me towards all the work I must accomplish and all the difficulties I must pass through. Grant that I may see You, even and above all, in the souls of my brothers, at their most personal, and most true, and most distant.

The gift which You call on me to make to these brothers—the only gift which my heart can make—is not the overwhelming tenderness of those specially privileged affections which You have placed in our lives as the most potent created factor of our inward growth, but something less sweet, but just as real, and more strong. Between myself and men, and with the help of Your Eucharist, You want the foundational attraction (which is already dimly felt in all love, if it is strong) to be made manifest—that which mystically transforms the myriad of rational creatures into a sort of single monad in You, Jesus Christ. You want me to be drawn towards 'the other,' not by simple personal sympathy, but by what is much higher: the united affinities of a world for itself and of that world for God.

You do not ask for the psychologically impossible—since what I am asked to cherish in the vast and unknown crowd is never anything save one and the same personal being which is Yours.

Nor do you call for any hypocritical protestations of love for my neighbour, because—since my heart cannot reach Your person except at the depths of all that is most individually and concretely personal in every 'other'—it is to the 'other' himself, and not to some vague entity around him, that my charity is addressed.

No, You do not ask anything false or unattainable of me. You merely, through Your revelation and Your grace, force what is most human in me to become conscious of itself at last. Humanity was sleeping—it is still sleeping—imprisoned in the narrow joys of its little closed loves. A tremendous spiritual power

*is slumbering in the depths of our multitude which will manifest
itself only when we have learnt to* break down the barriers *of
our egoisms and, by a fundamental recasting of our outlook,
raise ourselves up to the habitual and practical vision of universal realities.*

*Jesus, Saviour of human activity to which You have given
meaning, Saviour of human suffering to which You have given
living value, be also the Saviour of human unity; compel us to
discard our pettinesses, and to venture forth, resting upon You,
into the uncharted ocean of charity.*

iii. The outer darkness and the lost souls

The history of the Kingdom of God is, directly, one of a re-
union. The total divine milieu is formed by the incorporation
of every elected spirit in Jesus Christ. But to say "elect" is to
imply a choice, a selection. We should not be looking at the universal action of Jesus from a fully Christian point of view if it
were seen merely as a centre of attraction and beatification. It is
precisely because He is the One who unites that He is also the
One who separates and judges. The Gospel speaks of the good
seed, the sheep, the right hand of the Son of Man, the wedding
feast and the fire that kindles joy. But there are also the tares,
the goats, the left hand of the Judge, the closed door, the outer
darkness; and, at the antipodes of the fire that unites in love,
there is the fire that destroys in isolation. The whole process
out of which the New Earth is gradually born is an *aggregation*
increased two-fold by a *segregation*.

In the foregoing pages (solely concerned with rising towards
the divine Focus and with offering ourselves more completely
to its rays) our eyes have been systematically turned towards the
light, though we have never ceased to feel the darkness and the
void beneath us—the rarefication or absence of God over which
our path has been suspended. But this nether darkness, which

we sought to flee, could equally well have been a sort of abyss opening onto sheer nothingness. Imperfection, sin, evil, the flesh, appeared to us mainly as a retrograde step, a reverse aspect of things, which ceased to exist for us the further we penetrated into God.

Your revelation, O Lord, compels me to believe more. The powers of evil, in the universe, are not only an attraction, a deviation, a minus sign, an annihilating return to plurality. In the course of the spiritual evolution of the world, certain conscious elements in it, certain monads, deliberately detached themselves from the mass that is stimulated by Your attraction. Evil has become incarnate in them, has been 'substantialised' in them. And now I am surrounded by dark presences, by evil beings, by malign things, intermingled with Your luminous presence. That separated whole constitutes a definitive loss, an immortal wastage from the genesis of the world. There is not only nether darkness; there is also outer darkness. That is what the Gospels tell us.

Of the mysteries which we have to believe, O Lord, there is none, without a doubt, which so affronts our human views as that of damnation. And the more human we become, that is to say conscious of the treasures hidden in the least of beings and of the value represented by the smallest atom in the final unity, the more lost we feel at the thought of hell. We could perhaps understand falling back into inexistence . . . but what are we to make of eternal uselessness and eternal suffering?

You have told me, O God, to believe in hell. But You have forbidden me to hold with absolute certainty that a single man has been damned. I shall therefore make no attempt to consider the damned here, nor even to discover—by whatsoever means— whether there are any. I shall accept the existence of hell on Your word, as a structural element in the universe, and I shall pray and meditate until that awe-inspiring thing appears to me as a strengthening and even blessed complement to the vision of Your omnipresence which You have opened out to me.

And in truth, Lord, there is no need for me to force either my mind or things in order to perceive a source of life even in the mystery of that second death. We do not have to peer very closely into that outer darkness to discover in it a greater tension and a further deepening of Your greatness.

I know that the powers of evil, considered in their deliberate and malign action, can do nothing to trouble the divine milieu around me. As they try to penetrate into my universe, their influence (if I have enough faith) suffers the lot common to all created energy; caught up and twisted round by Your irresistible energy, temptations and evils are converted into good and fan the fires of love.

I know, too, that considered from the point of view of the void created by their defection from the Mystical Body, the fallen spirits cannot detract from the perfection of the Pleroma. Each soul that is lost in spite of the call of grace ought to spoil the perfection of the final and general union; but instead, O God, You offset it by one of those recastings which restore the universe at every moment to a new freshness and a new purity. The dammed are not excluded from the Pleroma, but only from its luminous aspect, and from its beatification. They lose it, but they are not lost to it.

The existence of hell, then, does not destroy anything and does not spoil anything in the divine milieu whose progress all around me I have followed with delight. I can even feel, moreover, that it effects something great and new there. It adds an accent, a gravity, a contrast, a depth which would not exist without it. The peak can only be measured from the abyss which it crowns.

I was speaking a moment or two ago—looking at things from

man's point of view—of a universe closed, from below, by nothingness, that is to say of a ladder of magnitudes that somehow
stops dead at zero. But now, O God, tearing open the nether
darkness of the universe, You show me that there is another
hemisphere at my feet—the very real domain, descending without end, of existences which are, at least, possible.

Does the reality of this negative pole of the world not double
the immensity and the urgency of the power with which You
come upon me?

O Jesus, our splendidly beautiful and jealous Master, closing
my eyes to what my human weakness cannot as yet understand
and therefore cannot bear—that is to say, to the reality of the
dammed—I desire at least to make the ever present threat of
damnation a part of my habitual and practical vision of the
world, not in order to fear You, but in order to be more intensely Yours.

Just now I besought You, Jesus, to be not only a brother for
me, but a God. Now, invested as You are with the redoubtable
power of selection which places You at the summit of the world
as the principle of universal attraction and universal repulsion,
You truly appear to me as the immense and living force which
I was seeking everywhere that I might adore it: the fires of hell
and the fires of heaven are not two different forces, but contrary
manifestation of the same energy.

I pray, O Master, that the flames of hell may not touch me
nor any of those whom I love, and even that they may never
touch anyone (and I know, my God, that you will forgive this
bold prayer); but that, for each and every one of us, their sombre
gleam may add, together with all the abysses that they reveal,
to the blazing plenitude of the divine milieu.

IN EXPECTATION OF THE
PAROUSIA

Segregation and aggregation. Separation of the evil elements of
the world, and 'co-adunation' of the elemental worlds that each
faithful spirit constructs around him in work and pain. Under
the influence of this two-fold movement, which is still almost
entirely hidden, the universe is being transformed and is maturing all around us.

We are sometimes inclined to think that the same things
are monotonously repeated over and over again in the history
of creation. That is because the season is too long by comparison
with the brevity of our individual lives, and the transformation
too vast and too inward by comparison with our superficial
and restricted outlook, for us to see the progress of what is
tirelessly taking place in and through all matter and all spirit.
Let us believe in Revelation, once again our faithful support in
our most human forebodings. Under the commonplace envelope
of things and of all our purified and salvaged efforts, a New Earth
is being slowly engendered.

One day, the Gospel tells us, the tension gradually accumu-
lating between humanity and God will touch the limits prescribed by the possibilities of the world. And then will come
the end. Then the presence of Christ, which has been silently
accruing in things, will suddenly be revealed—like a flash of light
from pole to pole. Breaking through all the barriers within

which the veil of matter and the water-tightness of souls have
seemingly kept it confined, it will invade the face of the earth.
And, under the finally liberated action of the true affinities
of being, the spiritual atoms of the world will be borne along
by a force generated by the powers of cohesion proper to the
universe itself and will occupy, whether within Christ or without Christ (but always under the influence of Christ), the place
of happiness or pain designated for them by the living structure
of the Pleroma. *Sicut fulgur exit ab Oriente et paret usque ad
Occidentem . . . Sicut venit diluvium et tulit omnes . . . Ita
erit adventus Filii hominis.* Like lightning, like a conflagration,
like a flood, the attraction exerted by the Son of Man will lay
hold of all the whirling elements in the universe so as to reunite
them or subject them to His body. *Ubicumque fuerit corpus
congregabuntur et aquilae.*

Such will be the consummation of the divine milieu.

As the Gospel warns us, it would be vain to speculate as
to the hour and the modalities of this formidable event. But
we have to *expect* it.

Expectation—anxious, collective and operative expectation of
an end of the world, that is to say of an issue for the world—
that is perhaps the supreme Christian function and the most
distinctive characteristic of our religion.

Historically speaking, that expectation has never ceased to
guide the progress of our faith like a torch. The Israelites were
constantly expectant, and the first Christians too. Christmas,
which might have been thought to turn our gaze towards the
past, has only fixed it further in the future. The Messiah who
appeared for a moment in our midst only allowed Himself to
be seen and touched for a moment before vanishing again,
more luminous and ineffable than ever, into the depths of the
future. He came. Yet now we must expect Him—no longer a
small chosen group among us, but all men—once again and

more than ever. The Lord Jesus will only come soon if we
ardently expect Him. It is an accumulation of desires that
should cause the Pleroma to burst upon us.

Successors to Israel, we Christians have been charged with
keeping the flame of desire ever alive in the world. Only twenty
centuries have passed since the Ascension. What have we made
of our expectancy?

A rather childish haste, combined with the error in perspective which led the first generation of Christians to believe in
the immediate return of Christ, has unfortunately left us disil-
lusioned and suspicious. Our faith in the Kingdom of God has
been disconcerted by the resistance of the world to good. A
certain pessimism, perhaps, encouraged by an exaggerated conception of the original fall, has led us to regard the world as
decidedly and incorrigibly wicked. And so we have allowed the
flame to die down in our sleeping hearts. No doubt we see with
greater or less distress the approach of individual death. No
doubt, again, our prayers and actions are conscientiously directed to bringing about 'the coming of God's Kingdom.' But
in fact how many of us are genuinely moved in the depths of
their heart by the wild hope that *our* earth will be recast? Who
is there who sets a course in the midst of our darkness towards
the first glimmer of a *real* dawn? Where is the Christian in
whom the impatient longing for Christ succeeds, not in sub-
merging (as it should) the cares of human love and human
interests, but even in counter-balancing them? Where is the
Catholic as passionately vowed (*by conviction* and not *by con-
vention*) to spreading the hopes of the Incarnation as are many
humanitarians to spreading the dream of the new city? We
persist in saying that we keep vigil in expectation of the Master.
But in reality we should have to admit, if we were sincere, *that
we no longer expect anything.*

The flame must be revived at all costs. At all costs we must renew in ourselves the desire and the hope for the great Coming. But where are we to look for the source of this rejuvenation? We shall clearly find it, first and foremost, in an increase of the attraction exercised directly by Christ upon His members. And then *in an increase of the interest,* discovered by our thought, in the preparation and consummation of the Parousia. And from where is this interest itself to spring? From the perception of *a more intimate connection* between the victory of Christ and the outcome of the work which our human effort here below is seeking to construct.

We are constantly forgetting that the supernatural is a ferment, a soul, and not a complete and finished organism. Its role is to transform 'nature'; but it cannot do so apart from the matter which nature provides it with. If the Jewish people have remained turned towards the Messiah for three thousand years, it is because He appeared to them to enshrine the glory of their people. If the disciples of St. Paul lived in perpetual expectation of the great day, that was because it was to the Son of Man that they looked for a personal and tangible solution to the problems and the injustices of life. The expectation of heaven cannot remain alive unless it is incarnate. What body shall we give to ours today?

That of a huge and *totally human* hope. Let us look at the earth around us. What is happening under our eyes within the mass of peoples? What is the cause of this disorder in society, this uneasy agitation, these swelling waves, these whirling and mingling currents and these turbulent and formidable new impulses? Mankind is visibly passing through a crisis of growth. Mankind is becoming dimly aware of its shortcomings and its capacities. And as we said on the first page, it sees the universe growing luminous like the horizon just before sunrise. It has a sense of premonition and of expectation.

Subject, like everyone else, to that attraction, the Christian, we said, sometimes wonders, and is uneasy. May he not be bestowing his adoration on an idol?

Our study, now completed, of the divine milieu suggests an answer to this fear.

Those of us who are disciples of Christ must not hesitate to harness this force, which needs us, and which we need. On the contrary, we should, under pain of allowing it to be lost and of perishing ourselves, share those aspirations, in essence religious, which make the men of today feel so strongly the immensity of the world, the greatness of the mind, and the sacred value of every new truth. It is in this way that our Christian generation will learn again to expect.

We have gone deeply into these new perspectives: the progress of the universe, and in particular of the human universe, does not take place in competition with God, nor does it squander energies that we rightly owe to Him. The greater man becomes, the more humanity becomes united, with consciousness of, and mastery of, its potentialities, the more beautiful creation will be, the more perfect adoration will become, and the more Christ will find, for mystical extensions, a body worthy of resurrection. The world can no more have two summits than a circumference can have two centres. The star for which the world is waiting, without yet being able to give it a name, or rightly appreciate its true transcendence, or even recognise the most spiritual and divine of its rays, is, necessarily, Christ Himself, in whom we hope. To desire the Parousia, all we have to do is to let the very heart of the earth, as we Christianise it, beat within us.

Men of little faith, why then do you fear or repudiate the progress of the world? Why foolishly multiply your warnings and your prohibitions? 'Don't venture . . . Don't try . . . everything is known: the earth is empty and old: there is nothing more to be discovered.'

We must try everything for Christ; we must hope everything for Christ. *Nihil intentatum.* That, on the contrary, is the true Christian attitude. To divinise does not mean to destroy, but to sur-create. We shall never know all that the Incarnation still expects of the world's potentialities. We shall never put enough hope in the growing unity of mankind.

Jerusalem, lift up your head. Look at the immense crowds of those who build and those who seek. All over the world, men are toiling—in laboratories, in studios, in deserts, in factories, in the vast social crucible. The ferment that is taking place by their instrumentality in art and science and thought is happening for your sake. Open, then, your arms and your heart, like Christ your Lord, and welcome the waters, the flood and the sap of humanity. Accept it, this sap—for, without its baptism, you will wither, without desire, like a flower out of water; and tend it, since, without your sun, it will disperse itself wildly in sterile shoots.

The temptations of too large a world, the seductions of too beautiful a world—where are these now?

They do not exist.

Now the earth can certainly clasp me in her giant arms. She can swell me with her life, or draw me back into her dust. She can deck herself with every charm, with every horror, with every mystery. She can intoxicate me with her perfume of tangibility and unity. She can cast me to my knees in expectation of what is maturing in her breast.

But her enchantments can no longer do me harm, since she has become for me, over and above herself, the body of Him who is and of Him who is coming.

The divine milieu.

Tientsin,
November 1926–March 1927.

Editor's Note.

In March 1955, the last month of his life among us, Father Teilhard de Chardin's thoughts went back to *The Divine Milieu*, and he wrote at the beginning of a final profession of faith:

'It is a long time now since, in *La Messe sur le Monde* and *Le Milieu Divin*, I tried to put into words the admiration and wonder I felt as I confronted perspectives as yet hardly formulated within me.

Today, after forty years of constant reflection, it is still exactly the same fundamental vision which I feel the need to set forth and to share, in its mature form, for the last time. With less exuberance and freshness of expression, perhaps, than at my first encounter with it, but still with the same wonder and the same passion.'

No work of this great believer can be understood except in relation to this 'fundamental vision' of *The Divine Milieu*—the vision (always implicit, even when not stated) of Christ as *All-in-everything*; of the universe moved and compenetrated by God in the totality of its evolution.

Because of this, the present publication throws a full light on *The Phenomenon of Man.*

TRANSLATIONS FROM THE LATIN

Page	Line	
101	32	Are turned into Christ
102	8	This is my Body
103	4	To subject all things to himself
	27	he descended to the lower regions
	32–33	Through whom, O God, thou dost always create, vivify and present all things to us
104	25	In Christ we live and move and have our being
105	17–18	How shall I comprehend as I am comprehended
106	7	Where shall I go from your spirit and where shall I flee from your face
	15–18	Neither death, nor life, nor angels, nor principalities, nor things present, nor things to come, nor powers, nor height, nor depth, nor any other creature
109	footnote	instinctively Christian
111	21–22	He created men . . . if perhaps they might draw (attract) him
	27	No one comes to me, unless the Father shall have drawn him
	30	Lord, make me see
	32	Brighten thy face above us
112	1	May the splendour of our God be above us
	4	Perfect spirit
	8	Send forth thy spirit and they shall be created and THOU SHALT RENEW THE FACE OF THE EARTH
	9	I work . . . the Father works always
114	27	Blessed art thou who hast believed
116	4	One jot or tittle shall not pass
117	10	Lord, help thou my unbelief
	30	This is my Body
	32	It is I, be not afraid
118	13	Faith, the substance of things
119	1–2	This is my food, to do the will of my Father
121	18–19	This it is that conquers the world, our faith
123	16	In the same house, many mansions
	20	That it become for us the Body and the Blood of our Lord Jesus Christ
124	11	This is my Body
134	9–11	Just as the lightning comes out of the east and appears even in the west . . . just as the flood comes and sweeps away all . . . so shall be the coming of the Son of Man
	14–15	Wherever the body shall be, there shall the eagles be gathered
138	2	nothing ventured

INDEX

Action, human: creative essence of, 32; detachment through, 40-43; fundamental law of, 24; meaning of, 31, 33-34; sanctification of, 18-19; *see also* Activity; Creation; Endeavour
Activity, human, 17, 18, 29; definition of, 17 n.; influence of passivities on, 46-47; syllogism of divinisation of, 25-31; will of God and, 22; *see also* Action; Creation; Endeavour
Adoration, meaning of, 107
Americanism, 86 n.
Angela of Foligno, 94
Annunciation, 114
Anthony, St., 84
Aquinas, St. Thomas, 67
Asceticism, 70, 74 n., 82
Attachment, *see* Detachment
Augustine, St., 17, 59

Baptism, 86

Charity, 124-128
Christian: duty of, 39; function of, 42; goal of, 42-43
Christianity: nature of, 39, 100; objection against, 37-38
Communion, 102, 105-106; *see also* Eucharist
Condemnation, doctrine of, 19
Creation, continuing nature of, 31, 79
Cross, meaning of, 76-79

Death, 54, 61, 91; *see also* Diminishment
Detachment, 19, 40-43, 55, 60, 67, 120; through attachment, 69-76; *see also* Development, human
Development, human, 17, 91; thwarts to, 47; *see also* Endeavour; Passivities of growth
Diaphany of the divine, 14 n., 110-112
Diminishment, meaning of, 60; misuse of, 73; divinisation of, 62; victory over, 54-55; *see also* Death; Passivities of diminishment

Divine milieu: charity and, 124-128; coming of, 108-110; consummation of, 134; energy in, 121; fundamental vision of, 139; individual value of, 121-123; man in, 93; nourishment of, 114; prayer and, 111; properties of, 92, 99; *see also* God, omnipresence of; Mysticism
Divine omnipresence, *see* God, omnipresence of
Divine will, 17 n., 23, 100; *see also* Activity, will of God and
Divinisation, 21, 23, 25, 33, 42, 54, 97, 116, 122, 123, 124, 138; *see also* Passivities; Passivities of growth; Salvation
Dualism, *see* Spiritual dualism
Duty, Christian, 71

Endeavour, 17, 21-22, 23, 33, 67; humanisation of, 37-40; sanctification of, 34-37; *see also* Action; Activity
Energies, *see* Energy
Energy, 17, 27-28, 36, 41, 47, 51, 62, 96, 114, 121
Eucharist, 102, 103, 104, 105; *see also* Communion
Evil, 52 n., 54, 55-61, 129-131

Faith, 114-118
Fidelity, 118-121
Francis, St., 97
Freedom, discipline of, 22

God: human progress and, 56; omnipresence of, 14-16, 31-34, 42-43, 57, 91, 100, 109, 111, 139; tangibility of, 15; *see also* Divine milieu
Good, capability for, 58
Gregory of Nyssa, St., 86
Growth, *see* Development, human; Passivities of growth

Incarnate word, *see* Incarnation